Alison Warp

632-4322

unscrupulous

Letting Go:
Uncomplicating
Your Life

Letting Go: Uncomplicating Your Life

Ramona Shepherd Adams

Herbert A. Otto

AuDeane Shepherd Cowley

MACMILLAN PUBLISHING CO., INC.

NEW YORK

Macmillan Publishing Co., Inc.
866 Third Avenue, New York, N.Y. 10022
Collier Macmillan Canada, Ltd.

Library of Congress Cataloging in Publication Data

Adams, Ramona Shepherd.
    Letting go.

    Bibliography: p.
    1. Success.   I.   Otto, Herbert Arthur, joint
author.   II.   Cowley, AuDeane Shepherd, joint
author.   III.   Title.
BF637.S8A28   158   80–318
ISBN 0–02–500270–8

---

10   9   8   7   6   5   4   3   2   1

Printed in the United States of America

Warning:

Reading this book
may prove to be
hazardous to
your current life-style
       which probably isn't
       as satisfying
       as it could be

If you are committed
to holding on
       to it
proceed with caution.

Contents

Introduction:
Why This Book
Came to Be

THIS BOOK WAS WRITTEN by three busy people who needed to uncomplicate their lives by "letting go." One of the authors, Dr. Adams, is a university dean, a therapist, a consultant, and a teacher. She is married, has a large family, and is involved in various community and professional activities. Dr. Otto is a psychologist, author, lecturer, and teacher. He was once a workaholic, with little time for his family and even less time for himself. The third, Dr. Cowley, is a professor at a school of social work, a marriage and family therapist, married, the mother of four children, and, when she finds time, a poet and a writer.

For several years, Dr. Adams and Dr. Cowley have been involved in teaching classes and conducting groups for students, including numerous older men and women who are seeking ways to refocus their lives and enrich their environment. Increasingly, both became aware that an underlying theme for many of the participants involved was the need to simplify their lives, to let go of a myriad of demands, expectations, compulsive behaviors, preconceived ideas, structured schedules, and programmed activities that cluttered and fragmented their lives.

As these concerns were discussed, the men and women volunteered more and more information about themselves. As the data increased, so did the descriptions of all the things in their lives that needed to be discarded, destroyed, or ignored if they were ever going to find time or energy to involve themselves in new activities and new life-styles.

Classes and group meetings were held on the University of Utah campus and at a YWCA community center. Each quarter the enrollments increased. There was a continuing pressure to spend more class time looking at ways these people could simplify their lives. Members of the class shared methods for simplifying and uncomplicating their lives. They made lists of things that they were doing to bring more order and sanity into their demanding schedules.

On analyzing the lists, some recurring themes surfaced. Most people needed to let go of their myths, their fantasies, their games, their security blankets, their outworn relationships, their unrealistic expectations, their irrational beliefs, and their focus on past experiences—which at this point had become only excess baggage. It seemed a logical deduction that, since these themes continued to reappear in various classes, perhaps they also were operating in the lives of people who would never have an opportunity to participate in such groups. A book focusing on the process of "letting go" suggested itself. At this point, Dr. Herbert Otto was contacted. He had been conducting classes and workshops for the development of personal potential for a number of years. He also had noted a need for participants of both sexes to focus on ways to uncomplicate their lives.

The idea of simplifying their lives is immediately appealing to those who feel they are living a rat race. Many colleges and universities as well as adult education programs offer classes and lecture series dedicated to enhancing the quality of life. But these classes seldom focus on ways to make life less complicated. This book focuses on that subject; it is an effort to share with you the experiences of class members who have grappled with the task of uncomplicating their own lives.

Letting go is a critical skill; therefore, *Letting Go* begins with the assumption that there can be too many pressures, responsibilities, and demands in life. This is followed by the process of setting new priorities that can simplify life, bring changes and personal growth. It is essential to possess this skill if we are to realize our possibilities and live life in its fullest measure. We are not born with this skill; we must learn it. We can learn it by reading about it, thinking about it, and practicing it. This book encourages the reader to do all three.

Letting Go: Uncomplicating Your Life

CHAPTER 1

Uncomplicating Your Life

ONE OF RALPH WALDO EMERSON'S FRIENDS once remarked to him, "The world is coming to an end tonight," to which Emerson replied, "That does not worry me. I can get along without it." In these words Emerson shared a great insight: The only way to enjoy something fully in life is to be able to part with it, to be able to let it go.

A Paradox

It is one of life's paradoxes that *you can fully enjoy only those things you are willing to let go.* If you think you cannot live without your youth, you will worry so much about growing old that you will not enjoy yourself even while young. If you believe you could not stand to live without good health, each minor ache or pain will create such fear and apprehension that you will not enjoy your health. If you feel you cannot live without your material possessions, you will monitor their use so closely and worry so about their safety that you will not enjoy them even in times of plenty.

Our sensitivity to the importance of letting things go is often dulled by our national preoccupation with acquiring more and more material possessions and worldly security. We work harder and harder to increase our gains and leave little time to considering how to use them. Instead of adding to our sense of enjoyment, these possessions often only add to our load of worries and concerns. We become dependent on them; we feel we could not live without them and begin to define ourselves by how many things we possess and how carefully we can keep them. Too often we fail to realize that this very fear of losing our possessions stems from feelings of insecurity that haunt us as we go about our daily task of acquiring more and more.

A successful forty-seven-year-old lawyer with five children experienced the drain that can accompany the ownership of material possessions. The upkeep of his country estate had required the purchasing of various machines, and the installation of systems to sprinkle the lawns, service the pools, and maintain the horses. In a Letting Go class discussing possessions, he described his frustrations as follows:

> Every time I buy something new, there goes one more slice of my energy to take care of it. It seems like all I do is repair or service one thing after another. Taking care of all these "things" keeps me so busy that I don't have any time to enjoy my home or my family. Every time I turn around I'm fixing something. Keeping all my equipment in working order is a job in itself!

Obviously, the solution would seem to be to get rid of some of those "work-savers." But according to that tired young lawyer, he couldn't get along without even *one* of them!

In dealing with our material possessions, and our interactions with the world, we sometimes get locked into an almost obsessive "holding on" with little awareness that our enjoyment of life and even our mental health may depend upon our ability to let go. In our attitudes and actions we also tend to crystallize our patterns of reacting and adopt a "once and for all" stance that makes no allowance for growth and change.

Rigidity Brings Stagnation

One common factor underlying human misery and lack of spontaneity is rigidity. The inability to change behavior patterns reflects a persistent and sometimes even pathological way of holding on to behaviors that don't work but instead cause pain. Many of our relationships and activities dull and eventually anesthetize our capacity to care. To save ourselves from stagnation, we literally have to rid ourselves of these destructive parts of ourselves.

Unfortunately, letting go is not a skill that is valued or often developed in our society. In fact, there is usually an immediate assumption that if we let something go, it is because it had no value or was a failure. This attitude was apparent in an exchange between two members of a Letting Go group. One member was describing a ranch in which she had invested, where women could go and find a haven for a few days of rest. She said the ranch had been in operation for nearly seven years but was now being closed. Another woman responded, "Oh, I'm so sorry it was a failure," to which she replied, "No, it was not a failure at all. It has simply accomplished its purpose."

It is unusual to find a person who is wise enough to let something go after it has accomplished its purpose. The more usual pattern is to collect. Our basements and attics are jammed full of things that no one will ever use again. They symbolize our need to hang on.

Excess Baggage

When the subject of letting go was discussed in our classes, all agreed immediately that there were many things in their lives that they would be better off without. However, most of them admitted they had never thought of letting them go. It was simply not an option they had considered.

These are some of the answers we received when we asked these same people to be more specific about the excess baggage in their lives:

• I've allowed other people's needs and requests to take too many blocks of my time.

• I've spent too much of my life in the pursuit of economic security, but I'm coming to feel that, given the state of the world today, there is no such thing as security. I need to pay more attention to *other* aspects of my life and let go of my consuming need to make money.

• I am too involved in my work. I can never leave it. I've got to learn to lock my brief case *inside* my office and let go of worries about work at five o'clock.

• I need to cut down on my community and church assignments. They put too much pressure on me.

• I've collected too many people to take care of. They depend on me and I allow them to use all my spare time. If I could let go of some of these unproductive relationships, I'd be able to find the time I keep looking for.

• I've got to let go of my habit of worrying about things I can't do anything about. I'm constantly thinking about my father who lives alone in Florida, my sister who's a widow, and my grandchildren. I'm always consumed with anxiety about them, and I can't *do* anything. It leaves me exhausted.

Recent research underscores the fact that an incredible amount of energy is used in unproductive ways. It is generally accepted that most people are functioning at only 4 to 10 percent of their potential. Our potential is dissipated by excessive pressures, responsibilities, and demands. *Uncomplicating your life is one of the first steps in personal growth* and yet most people find it difficult to engage in the process of simplifying.

> Simplify, simplify. Instead of three meals a day, if it be necessary eat but one; instead of a hundred duties, five; and reduce other things in proportion.   .
>
> —Henry David Thoreau

Growing Pains

We accept the principle that "growing" implies "outgrowing" when applied to the clothes we wear, but reject the implication when it is applied to ideas, patterns of behavior, relationships, and our sense of self. Leaving behind or moving beyond the familiar is often viewed as a frightening venture fraught with many dangers. Small wonder that so many choose to avoid the pain and work of growth by hanging on to the safety of the status quo.

Praise and support from friends or significant others are sometimes available if we do well in those traditional and accepted tasks that society expects of us. But our most difficult task—self-actualization—often must be accomplished without support or even *against* the wishes of those who have an interest in our lives.

A class member who faced this situation commented:

When I started to uncomplicate my life, my family and others close to me started to raise objections. They resisted my efforts to make personal changes by documenting a million reasons why I should stay the same. They felt my style at forty should be the same as it had been at twenty, even though I had raised three children, survived two wars, earned two college degrees, met new friends, and found new values. What I saw as growth, they saw as destructive change. They were threatened. They punished: They said I was selfish, that I was thinking only of myself. They questioned my loyalties. They made me feel guilty. They judged by their standards. They gave no support. I ended up feeling abandoned and alone in my efforts to grow. The things about me that I had come to value the most, and had achieved at no small effort, were the very things they most devalued.

For a while, I kept hoping they would understand. Now I realize that they may never understand, because the things I care about are not the same as the things they think I *should* care about. Now I know that my only hope is to protect myself from their negative criticisms and to have faith in the fact that for the first time in five years I can sleep without pills and begin my days without tears and depression.

To become a self-actualized, or authentic, person is discussed widely and recognized as a goal worth seeking. But how seriously does our society, dominated as it is by unauthentic relationships, reward the seeker? We get two different messages from our culture: One says, "actualize"; the other, "conform." Few prizes are given to the person who is spontaneous, detached, autonomous, and loyal to universal rather than local values, a person able to resist conforming to the lowest common denominator. In fact, those who *do* conform to the lowest common denominator are often rewarded because the lowest common denominator reflects the values of the majority. But, the fact that the majority shares a value does not mean that the value facilitates personal growth. Although there is power in numbers, this type of power is not necessarily rational or constructive.

Edward R. Murrow once observed, "We live in a time when the tide runs toward the shore of conformity." In daily life conformity, consistency, and predictability are often valued over creativity, spontaneity, and imagination. The person who follows convention garners more rewards in the short run than the person who accepts conventions only if they have passed the test of personal relevancy. The self-actualized person must at times tread life's paths alone, with little support.

Finding New Options

It is common to hear colleagues and friends complain about the frenetic pace of their days, their lack of time for the things that matter most, and their resigned bitterness about the lack of quality in their days . . . and weeks . . . and years. Too often such a waste of time and human potential is not only tolerated but accepted. "That's the way life is," they say, and few even pause to consider that one need not deny one's secret desires; that there are ways to organize life more productively; that one can control what does and does not consume one's life.

Occasionally a courageous example disturbs a bored, complacent, robotized way of life. You might hear about a friend who withdrew part of a retirement fund he had labeled "for the future," and took a trip just for the enjoyment of it. You might be tempted when you learn that someone you know has simply chucked it all and gone to Alaska to fish. You like the feel of it. You honor the person who has the courage to chuck it, but you usually end up with numerous reasons for not doing the same thing.

Maybe you once read about an adventurous woman who visited an island paradise, responded to it from some deep core of being, and instead of saying, "I love it here," and then returning home, decided to uproot her comparatively humdrum existence and begin anew, actually daring to adopt an entirely new life-style.

Or, perhaps you heard from an old friend who wrote that he had sold his townhouse, bought acreage in the country, quit his job, and devised a system for physical survival that required he work only one day a week, six months of the year, leaving the rest of his time open for what he described as "blocks of time for living." When one is brought face to face with such examples of people who seem to have a unique way of life, it shocks and even disturbs. We are not consoled to realize that life is what we decide to make it, particularly if we feel *we* are not getting enough out of it.

Sometimes, before we can build, we must tear down an old structure, or at least move it aside. In his book *Art of Life*, Havelock Ellis describes this process:

> We cannot count too precious in any age those who sweep away outworn traditions, effete routines, the burden of unnecessary duties and superfluous luxuries and useless moralities, too heavy to be borne. We rebel against these rebels, even shudder at the sacrilegious daring, but, after all, they are a part of life, an absolutely necessary part of it. For life is a breaking down as well as a building up (Ellis 1929, p. 123).

Uncomplicating your life by discarding the unnecessary and the negative is the first step toward further personal growth and the actualizing of your own unique potential. To seekers and searchers interested in this quest, there is a happy note. In contradiction to all we have heard in our consumer-oriented society, getting there seems to be dependent *not* on what you have but on what you are willing to give up and *let go.*

How to Get the Most from This Book

This is a book both for reading and for doing. If you are not particularly interested in taking action, merely reading will give you access to a new perspective, to a new philosophy and attitude toward letting go and uncomplicating your life. If you are on the other hand a person interested in doing something about life's pressures and complications, you will enjoy the many detailed prescriptions for action described in each chapter.

You may wish to begin by using the Letting Go Analysis Chart. This chart is designed to help you select priorities, to determine what particular areas you feel are important to you, and to help you decide where you want to begin the adventure of letting go.

LETTING GO ANALYSIS CHART

AREA	DEGREE TO WHICH I NEED TO LET GO			
	None	*Little*	*Some*	*Much*
Letting Go of Outside Pressures				
Letting Go of Tired Relationships				
Letting Go of the Past				
Letting Go of Security Blankets				
Letting Go of Myths and Fantasies				
Letting Go of Games and Artificiality				
Letting Go of Constrictive Personal Habits				

Place check marks in the appropriate columns above.

CHAPTER 2

Letting Go
of Outside Pressures

EXCESSIVE AND COMPETING DEMANDS can fragment our days and make deep erosions in our lives. A forty-eight-year-old career woman shared the following with a Letting Go class:

> Though I am cheered by the crowd for all my accomplishments, I find it hard to figure out what they are cheering about. It's true I've been busy all my life accomplishing things, but at forty-eight I wonder what accomplishment *really* is. I just feel pressured and pressed. There's no time for genuine relationships; and, if I had time, I'm not really sure I'd know how to go about making any good ones anymore. I've always used my work as an escape from solving my personal problems, and I've just gone from one assignment to another never leaving any time to think about why I'm doing it all. It's crazy.
>
> It doesn't make any sense when you think about it, but who's ever had time to think about it? I certainly haven't. There have been so many competing projects in my life that have had no pay-offs for anyone. I just wish I'd been smart enough to give a lot of them up when I was younger. My life would be better today if I had. Now I must begin to let go of many of my projects. Whether I like it or not, I must admit that I have to slow down. If I'd done it earlier in my life I probably wouldn't be feeling such an internal collapse now.

A double bind conflict faces men and women in our culture as they are forced to choose between competing and often mutually exclusive values. Which will it be—success in the home or success on the job? They are pushed to excel in desk-bound jobs and still keep in good physical condition, to maintain interpersonal sensitivity and yet be aggressive enough to produce, to be sensitive and yet to maintain a stoic stance.

Men and women are pushed to develop talents, to support church activities, to be politically active, and to exercise their minds and bodies. We all get caught in the business of it all. Seldom can we find the time between one demand and another to stop the feverish pace and wonder about who we are and what we are doing. There is little time for sorting and therefore no rational criteria for letting go. We become more and more fragmented and less and less satisfied with the quality of our lives.

A forty-year-old man who had "made it" professionally and who only four weeks before had been awarded his community's highest honor, that of "successful businessman of the year," said:

> I wonder what it's all about. It seems to me that life is just a continual round of demands. There are deadlines to meet, bills to pay, responsibilities to perform, people who depend on you, and no place to turn for relief. Sometimes I feel desperate. I want to escape. I want to leave everything—let it all go—and just get away where no one knows me and there's time to think. Sometimes I feel like I'd risk everything—my marriage, my children, my home, my job, my friends, *everything*—for a chance to get a second breath. It's a crazy paradox because in letting go of all those things I would be emptying my life of the very things I love and cherish most and for which I have worked the hardest. I've got to let go of something, but there isn't even a letup in the pressure so I can figure out what should go! All I know is that the way I'm living now is breaking my back and destroying my spirit.

Before it is too late, this man may realize that unless he makes a conscious decision to give up some of the less important things in his life, he may, in some not too distant future, be forced to give up all the things he cares about, both the important and the unimportant. To wait for the time when mounting pressures will force his hand and leave him no rational choice makes no sense at all, as illustrated by the following case history.

A fifty-year-old lawyer shared with a Letting Go class the story of how he was "forced" to slow down:

> It wasn't easy. For too many years I ignored things I cared about for things I didn't care about at all. I tried to meet every demand that people made on my time. The pressure was getting me down and I almost lost my position and my family before poor health *forced* me to take a look at my frenetic, fragmented schedule. I had known for a long time that my crowded schedule made no sense. Each day I could feel my life being drained out of me, but I didn't know how to stop. I felt empty and tired. I lacked spontaneity and motivation. Life seemed increasingly like a drag I could do without.
>
> Poor health is what *made* me confront head-on my foolish behavior. It made me stop for a while. It gave me time to think. As I lay waiting for strength to ebb back into my body I realized I had never really done my "own" thing. How could I have done it? I didn't even know what my own thing was. I had never taken time to define it.

Taking Time to Think

Members of a Letting Go class were asked to write in no more than two sentences about the nature of their outside pressures and demands. Some of the results follow:

> Pressures come from my work (some of which I take home); my wife (who wants me to fix things around the home); my children (who want Daddy's attention); my acquaintances and neighbors (to whom we owe invitations); and even my dog (he always needs to be taken for a walk). Add to these pressures the calls and demands from parents and relatives who live in town and you may get some idea of why I feel so hassled.

Another student said:

> I trace my pressures to the three-bedroom home I have to run without any help from my four young children or my husband, and the

nosy "friends" I've got. Last but not least, I've got no one to talk to and that creates the worst pressure of all.

Another said:

My pressures and demands come from family, too much social life, too much chauffeuring of kids, too many community meetings, and too many church committees. The worst pressure for me I think is lack of privacy. I have no time for myself because either the kids want something or the phone is ringing.

How do you find time among all the demands? Where should your loyalties go? Out of a twenty-four-hour day, most people find ten hours or more going to the area of work. If you figure eight hours of sleep, eating, etc., then you have approximately six hours left to divide between the responsibilities of family, the other people who matter, all your extracurricular activities—and yourself. It sounds like enough, but it never is. What if you were to end up at the close of a day with six hours available? What would you do with them? Would you know how to use them productively even if they were available, or has your fragmentation become so institutionalized that you'd be at a loss as to how to use your newfound free time?

There are three main dimensions in life: home; work; and extracurricular. Each of these contributes its share of pressures and demands. We all need to analyze the nature of these pressures and take steps to lessen them.

Perhaps the first step in letting go is to question why you are so pressured and have so little time. By raising questions, change is often initiated and pressures reduced. New perspectives often lead to new ways of coping. If you can make even one change, the domino effect is often set in motion so that as you eliminate one pressure, others can be made to topple also.

Pressure Diagnosis

It is important to identify the specific nature and form of your outside pressures. Many people are quite aware of being "under pressure" from external sources, but they have little idea about how to alleviate these pressures and often they are vague about where the pressures are originating. Irene R., a woman with a demanding profession, explained: "I have the feeling that the pressures on me have been getting worse over the last two years. I couldn't tell you why or what they are, but I feel it." Some people may have a vague, generalized sense of being pressured, but far too few have ever taken a clear look at the broad range of factors and forces that produce these pressures. That is unfortunate, because *coping with pressures and demands begins with identifying them.* A two-step sequence in the pressure-diagnosis process is helpful: (1) the Total Pressure Drawing, and (2) the Identification of Pressure Sources and Intensities.

The Total Pressure Drawing

Begin by drawing yourself in the middle of a sheet of paper. Now show the pressures and demands that are coming at you from all sides by using arrows of different size and thickness to indicate the intensity of the identified pressures. Label these pressures. Draw them as symbols and illustrate their impact on you in whatever way seems appropriate. Surprisingly, new insights and awareness often occur even during the process of drawing.

In the course of sketching out the nature of her pressures, Judy S. commented to her neighbor, "Look at the heavy arrows I drew from the dogs to myself. I am suddenly in touch with how much I resent taking care of my husband's dogs! It's all on *my* shoulders."

Max L., a middle-aged leader in his profession, noted, "As I drew the connections between myself and all those offices and obligations I took on in various professional societies, I noticed a distinctly oppressive feeling that I had not been aware of before. I'm suddenly realizing that week after week I don't need the pressure of putting out that newsletter."

Do your own Pressure Drawing. Be spontaneous and draw it

without thinking too much about it. Be sure to include as many pressures and demands as you feel right now. When you finish, look at the drawing. What did you leave out? What does it tell you? Have you clearly labeled and identified all the pressures of which you are presently aware, or can you think of others that should be added? Add to the drawing until you feel confident that you can identify no more. Now put the drawing away in a drawer or file.

Let a day or two elapse *after* the completion of your Pressure Drawing. You will then be ready for the detailed identification of the pressure sources and intensities. You may want to share your drawing with someone with whom you can talk honestly and candidly about the pressures in your life. Ideally, this will be someone you trust. It should be someone who cares about you and is able and interested in helping you to evaluate your drawing. He or she may see things you didn't—or have additional suggestions to offer from a more objective point of view. To identify and share perceptions with such a helping person is important, because it is so easy to lose perspective when trying to deal with your own problems.

A class member shared the following observation: "I asked my best friend to help me diagnose the pressure patterns in my own life. I'm really glad I did because he pointed out blind spots, important things I had 'forgotten' to put on the list—like duty visits to my in-laws. He also gave me many other valuable ideas."

Finally, we need to remember that it is important not to begin talking to a helpful friend or anyone else until you have finished both the Pressure Drawing and your own work on the Identification of the Pressure Sources and Intensities. To seek help before you have wrestled with the configuration yourself bypasses a critical step in the process.

Identification of the Pressure Sources and Intensities

Take three separate sheets of paper. On one sheet write the heading "Home Pressures and Demands." On another sheet write "Work Pressures and Demands," and on the third sheet write "Extracurricular Pressures and Demands." Now, *without* consulting your Total Pressure Drawing take each sheet in turn and list as rapidly as possible all the pressures and demands that belong under each category.

When you have completed this task as thoroughly as you can, find your Total Pressure Drawing and compare it with your three lists. If you have noted some pressures and demands on your drawing that do not appear on your lists, add those to the lists now. Conversely, add to your three lists any of the pressures and demands noted on your drawing that may have been left out of your lists.

Now, using the Total Pressure Drawing as your guide, compare the arrows or symbols that you have drawn. Which ones expressed greater intensity or force? Which ones seem relatively unimportant? Look over each list carefully and from each one select the three items that you feel account for the strongest pressures on you. Rank them from one to three, with one indicating the strongest pressure. You have now identified what you feel are the nine strongest demands and pressures in your life. Questions like the following can be useful as you discuss various areas.

HOME

How do you use your time while at home?

How much of what you do at home is valuable to you?

How much of what you do is not productive?

How many of the personally unsatisfying tasks that you now do could be delegated to others?

Are there ways you can stretch your time at home by getting up earlier or staying up later?

How can you organize to better advantage the time you now have available?

WORK

Do you allow yourself to be distracted and fragmented at work? For example, do you allow people to interrupt you, to drop in without an appointment?

Would a meeting with a colleague or someone in a supervisory capacity be helpful in clarifying where you might direct more of your energies to accomplish your goals on the job?

Are there any committees or duties you can shift up or down or across the organizational ladder?

Are there resources available in your organization which you are not using that might save you time and energy?

Do you have options and leeway in your schedule and activities that you are not utilizing?

Can you think of ways you could work more efficiently on your own or, conversely, with colleagues?

EXTRACURRICULAR

Have you ever taken a look at how much time you spend on extracurricular activities? How many outside activities are you trying to do?

Do you like the way you spend your free time? Did you choose what you would do in your spare time? Or have many of your hours been filled by things you would prefer not to do, because you find it difficult to say no?

How much of your time is used for fun and relaxation and how much is devoted to obligations?

If you don't have a good balance between fun and relaxation and other things that demand your time, how can you establish such a balance?

Is there anything that you could change or drop in order to lessen demands and pressures?

As a final step in letting go of outside pressures and demands you will want to look over some of the suggestions found on the following pages. Mark the ones that sound most interesting and helpful. Then proceed to utilize them!

Contributions, Suggestions, and Ideas from Letting Go Groups and Classes

Over a period of time we asked members in Letting Go classes to make short reports on what they had done to reduce pressures at work, at home, and in the extracurricular area. We also asked them to write out any ideas they had that would reduce demands and pressures. You may find some of these ideas and suggestions very useful and directly applicable to your own situation.

HOME PRESSURES AND DEMANDS

IDEA.   Why not begin by sharing with your husband/wife/ children/roommate what you feel are the major pressures and demands in your home? Ask them for help. Though this may be difficult, remember that living with these pressures may consume much more of your energy than it will take to deal with them.

> I used to feel the necessity to say "yes" to most demands from children, husband, church workers, or what have you. I would feel guilty if I didn't take on what people asked me to do. Now I've completely turned myself around. I say "yes" to very little and most of the pressures are gone!

IDEA.   Home has often been depicted in literature as "our haven for rest" or the "port which protects us from life's difficult storms." For most of us, however, home is an area where there are many ongoing and unresolved pressures and demands. Because it is so often described in idealistic terms, it makes us hesitant to admit, even to ourselves, that we have not managed to bring such peace and contentment into our family. As a result, there may be feelings of guilt and the fear that we are incompetent. This fear and guilt may be robbing us of energy and isolating us from resources that could be useful in helping to eliminate pressures.

We are under financial pressure. To meet this problem head-on, we called a family council meeting and talked it over. It was helpful to get everyone's opinion. We now have some good ideas on how to cut corners and save. The two girls even came up with some ideas on how they could make money. We are taking a good look at that. The result is that we are pulling together now—and many of the pressures which were causing problems are being eliminated.

IDEA.   If some of the pressures are being generated by financial considerations and obligations, there are a number of alternatives that can be useful. If budgeting is a problem, ask for assistance in establishing a realistic budget. You may need some outside help to accomplish this task. Perhaps you do not really know good budgeting procedure. There are a number of valuable resources available in most communities. Five possible sources of budget information are:

1. Financial advisers who have professional skills in solving money problems. These advisers are listed in the Yellow Pages.

2. The Bureau of Labor Statistics focuses on the development of budget information that can be used to inform agencies and individuals about the trends in our economy. If you want some specific information in planning home budgets, write and ask for information dealing with that particular subject.

3. Many insurance companies have tables showing families how budgets can be made and used more effectively.

4. Home economics departments in major universities will also send such information upon request.

5. There are often good resources among friends and acquaintances. If you inquire, you can probably find people you know and trust who would be willing to share their skills and experiences with you.

When our family met around our financial problem, we found these questions to be most important. In order of importance they are: 1) In what new ways can income be generated? 2) What luxuries can be cut? 3) How can we allocate and use our present income?

My fourteen-year-old girl said, "The energy we would have spent worrying we are now spending on looking for some good answers." This has created a decidedly more positive attitude in all of us.

IDEA.   Where in your busy schedule can you find spaces that can be used to replenish the energy that you use in the course of your daily tasks? Anne Morrow Lindbergh describes the need for this replenishing process in these words:

> Total retirement is not possible. I cannot shed my responsibilities. I cannot permanently inhabit a desert island. I cannot be a nun in the midst of my family life. I would not want to be. The solution for me, surely, is neither in total renunciation of the world, nor in total acceptance of it. I must find a balance somewhere, or an alternating rhythm between these two extremes; a swinging of the pendulum between solitude and return. In my periods of retreat, perhaps I can learn something to carry back into my worldly life. (Lindbergh 1955, p. 30).

If you can't take a vacation or a weekend off, find a few hours during the week that you can label as your own. Don't use these hours to mow the lawn, complete reports, pick up the laundry you forgot last Thursday, do income tax returns, or to take the children's shoes to be fixed. These ar *your* hours for personal regeneration. Do with them something that is special for you. *You need to fill your own cup.* Filling your own cup is a critical task because you can never meet any one else's needs until you have met your own. You will be surprised at how much energy will be generated just by anticipating a chance to do something you really want to do!

> The best idea I ever had was to organize a car pool. Taking the children everywhere took so much time. I got five people to join the pool. Now, each is responsible for one day of chauffeuring. I learned from this class and resisted the temptation to fill up the time I had saved with other tasks. Instead, my extra time is used for

relaxation and pleasurable experiences for myself. You can't imagine how I look forward to this "free" time!

IDEA. Create a similar shared arrangement for tending baby or heavy yard work. Work out a schedule of mutually advantageous exchange with your friends and neighbors. Not only would it give you an added resource but it could save you money as well. It's worth a try! Other responsibilities and chores around the house can also be shared:

We used to have Sunday evening as the time when everyone fixed his/her own meal. This was a tradition with a lot of families. Then, one time when we were all together I proposed Wednesday night, when some of us are busy, as another "fix your own meal" evening. All week I find myself looking forward to Wednesday as well as Sunday.

IDEA. If household management and care is a source of pressure, have you tried:

• Scheduling specific tasks to be done by specific family members on certain days?

• Letting other family members assume some of the supervisory or upkeep tasks instead of your feeling the responsibility for supervising everything that needs to happen in the home? Letting go of some tasks not only frees you but gets others involved in ways that help them to feel more a part of the home.

• Having a scheduled two-hour workfest once every week or two? During the workfest *everyone* would be expected to work. Refreshments could be served and an air of celebration generated from the activities. You'll be surprised how much this gets done!

• Fighting household boredom by working out a system of rotating specific household chores? This would free everyone from routine demands.

WORK PRESSURES AND DEMANDS

I used to take home feelings and pressures that had accumulated at work and "unload" them on my wife. You can imagine the results.

I finally thought of taking my tape recorder to the bedroom and having a yelling and shouting session with it. I listened to the playbacks and found them very helpful in critiquing my concerns and giving me new ideas on how to solve some of the problems which were pressing in upon me. From the first day I tried this—we've had a better marriage!

IDEA. Do a time study of your on-the-job functions. Keep careful notes for a week documenting when and how you spend blocks of time. At the end of the week analyze your schedule and weed out the unproductive activities.

Then establish a new system of priorities in your work.

I had some terrific results from asking my secretary and some of the other people in my office for ideas on reducing work pressures.

IDEA. Your style of communication may have something to do with the pressures you are experiencing on your job. A great deal of energy is wasted in solving personal misunderstandings and on-the-job problems created by inadequate or misunderstood communication. Identify what consistently creates problems for you with others because of your style of communicating. Ask yourself about the frequency of your communication. Is it frequent enough? Is it too open or too guarded? Do you tend to put too much or too little in writing? Is there too much or too little oral communication? Get an outside opinion, or even take a communication course if necessary.

One of the most valuable things I got out of this class was the suggestion to take a communication course. I am halfway through it now and can already see the results in my work.

IDEA. Take an inventory of your talents, skills, and resources. Do you have some that you have not been using in your work? We tend to compartmentalize our skills and see certain ones as applicable only to work and others applicable only to activities at home, at school, or in the community. Can you see how you can apply more of your "at home or play" skills to your work, or vice versa?

I started using my office organizing skills in my volunteer activity—and I was surprised to see how much time I saved the first week.

IDEA. One of the best ways to deal more effectively with job pressures and demands is by creating new energy and vitality in your own life. New energy and vitality are generated through involvement in activities and interests that are satisfying for *you*. They come from a change of pace or a good rest. Give yourself that long weekend of fun and rest you have been promising yourself or, even better, take a week or two to regenerate your energy. Use the energy accumulated during this time to deal with work demands. Such a periodic change of pace is not a luxury. It is a necessity if you want to keep your energy levels at their maximum.

I've always been against list making. I guess it was a reaction to my mother, who made them all the time. My greatest discovery for reducing job pressures was making a list of what needed to be done *every morning* and then thinking through the priorities. This actually gave me some time I never would have had!

EXTRACURRICULAR PRESSURES AND DEMANDS

Many times social obligations seem to loom larger than they really are because there is no clear awareness of how extensive they are. Also, usually the postponed obligations create the pressures. All social obligations can be divided into three time-related categories:

• Current—You feel you need to or want to see someone, but there is no particular pressure to do this.
• Past due—There is some pressure because you should have attended to this or that with a person.
• Way past due—These are really bothersome as they have been postponed and really need to be given some attention.

Do you have a clear idea of the nature of *your* social obligations? What precisely are they? Getting them down on a piece of paper is helpful. The following two lists are examples made by members of Letting Go classes:

Henry B.'s List	*Sally K.'s List*
Lunch with Jim (way past due)	Call Jane R. (past due)
Lunch with Harold	Call Mary (current)
Get together with Donald R. (past due)	Call Frank B. (way past due)
Invite Sam and Helen R. to house (past due)	Visit Betty (way past due)
Invite the Kellys to house (way past due)	Visit Mrs. L. (way past due)
Lunch with Mr. D. (current)	Lunch at club with Charles and Betty (current)
Lunch with Bruce D., Mac L. (current)	Lunch with Helen (way past due)
	Dinner with McFarlands (past due)
	Call Harry for appointment (past due)

The comments of both persons who compiled the above lists are revealing. Henry B. told class members, "Making the list motivated me. I cleared with my wife and called the two people marked 'past due.'" Sally K. reported, "I had let the social obligations pile up. There were so many and I was so far behind. I was immobilized. What a relief to get it down on paper. It's a long list, but half the pressure is gone because now I'm going to do something about it!"

IDEA. Take a look at how you spend your fun and recreation time. How many of these activities yield low-level fun or are no fun at all? Concentrate on those recreational activities that give you considerable pleasure and joy. Let the rest go.

IDEA. It is one of the paradoxes of our time that social parties and gatherings that should be a source of enjoyment, fun, relaxation, and recreation all too often add to the pressures, artificialities, and discomforts of contemporary life. The challenge is to reverse this process. More people today are planning joint parties with friends or neighbors. The idea is to share in preparations and costs and offer guests an opportunity to meet some new people. Be sure to talk about all aspects of co-hosting before the party. Co-hosting usually means more time to *enjoy* the party and less work for the hosts.

The Organizational Involvement Analysis

Many of us are "overorganized"—we belong to too many organizations, clubs, and special groups. These make demands on our time, and they take energy. To remedy this situation, try an Organizational Involvement Analysis.

> For years I've been griping to my friends about all the meetings I have to attend. They used to kid me. "Susan, you love it!" they said. The truth is I just got caught and then accepted it. When I heard Louise say she was in too many organizations (and she was only in three), the bells tolled for me. I used the organizational involvement analysis idea and this took off about 90 percent of the pressures on me.

Try it yourself! Make a list of all the organizations, clubs, professional groups, sports groups, etc., to which you belong. Next, rank them, asking yourself, "Which organizations are most important to me?" Also, note if there are any on the list that have lost their appeal or usefulness in your life. Finally, rewrite your list according to the priorities you have established, placing the most important organization first. Now, drop membership in the organization(s) lowest on your priority list.

To continue the process of uncomplicating your life, consult your priority list and note how much time per month you are devoting to each organization. Include travel time to meetings and any time you may spend preparing for them. Based on the time spent on each organization, decide (1) which organizations to drop, and (2) how to cut down on the time you devote to the organizations you decide to keep on your active list.

You may choose to phase out gently your membership in an organization by attending fewer and fewer meetings. Declare this intention to those in the organization who need to know. The

gentle phaseout helps prevent negative feelings by members of
the organization and gives you a chance to test your feelings
about the value of the organization to your life overall. As a
part of this phaseout process, you may want to arrange having
a personal representative attend meetings for you a few times.
This is also a way of making known your intention of withdraw-
ing from the organization, and it could help you decide if missing
the meetings leaves a gap in your life. The only way you can rid
yourself of those activities that dilute and waste your energies
is to let them go.

Making It "In" to Drop Out

Escaping into activities has become a way of life today for far
too many of us. Fragmented and pulled in every direction, we
arm ourselves against the fear of vulnerability with masks and
facades, games, and imposed agendas. We become too busy to
know ourselves and hence we cannot share ourselves with anyone else. If perpetuated, this life-style can lead to a kind of
personal isolation. When we allow our time to be used up by
outside activities, none is left over during which to create meaningful relationships. Intimacy cannot be made of leftovers.

Letting go of outside pressures can be one of the less difficult
and more rewarding ways of uncomplicating your life. It is
rewarding because considerable blocks of free time are recovered
and a new feeling of freedom is created.

You can add *years* to your life by salvaging precious hours
daily!

Finding the balance that works for *you* is another subject in
which you are the only expert.

CHAPTER 3

Letting Go
of Tired Relationships

ANN S. IS BUSY managing her household of a husband, three children, and two pets. She has been trying to sell real estate on a part-time basis and this is a particularly busy morning. Ann is waiting for a call from a real estate broker. The phone rings, and it is Beth, a friend from her early college days. They had lost touch for many years but now Beth was calling to tell Ann that she had moved to a small town just two hours away.

On the phone Beth is her usual breathless self, impatient to tell Ann the latest gossip. "I just can't wait to talk to you. It's been so long since we've seen each other." Without pausing she continues, "What have you heard about the old crowd? Did you know I finally got in touch with Jane? Will you be surprised to hear what *she* has to say!"

Ann sighs impatiently. She knows she is condemned to a long phone session unless she agrees to have lunch. Ann is keenly aware that she and Beth have little in common other than talk about people from the past. "How can I get rid of Beth? I don't really want to see her," she asks herself while half listening to the voice on the phone.

Most of us tend to maintain connections with people although we are past the point of caring about the relationship, which now has little or no meaning for us. We are also prone to hold on to some "unhealthy" relationships that stunt our emotional growth. These are the *tired relationships* that clutter our lives. Habit, inertia, fatigue, or lack of awareness that a relationship has largely lost its meaning, or is in fact damaging us, keep us from terminating it. These tired relationships keep us constricted and prevent new relationships from developing and adding new vitality to our lives. Awareness of the types of tired relationships that abound is one way to begin the process of letting them go.

Some Types of Tired Relationships

The type of tired relationship that is the most difficult to recognize and that is consistently ignored is the *control relationship*. Manipulation of one person by another is the main characteristic in this type of relationship. Both the manipulator and the manipulated are often unaware of this main theme in their responses to each other. Usually there is at least minimal mutual satisfaction with the nature of their interaction. Paradoxically, however, on some level or another both participants are aware that this relationship is not healthy in all respects. The controller and the controlled recognize that, at best, the relationship has limited value and duration. Because it provides certain satisfactions for both and is supported by the structures of our authority-centered culture, which encourages dependencies, the control relationship is both difficult to recognize and hard to terminate. But it can happen!

During a group discussion describing the "control relationship" Tom blurted out:

> I didn't realize until just now that I've been in one of those. Jack is my best friend. We met in the army. He's always given me advice on what to do. If I have any questions about anything I go see him. He's really been the leader and I the follower. "Control" might be too strong a word—but then again, maybe it's not!

The *possessive relationship* is so widespread and universally accepted that it is almost a norm. This fact, however, does not diminish its basically pernicious and destructive nature. In some ways the possessive type of relationship is close to the control type. It flourishes especially in man/woman and parent/child relationships. Husbands believe and act as if they "own" their wives, and vice versa. We continually hear such statements as "my wife knows that whatever she wants to do is usually OK as long as she checks with me first," "my husband *let* me go on the trip," "he always *allows* me to do what I want to do," "I can't stand men who ogle women. It took me a while to break my husband of the habit, but he's all *mine* now." Many parents believe and act as if children were indeed their private possessions. Again, some, if not all, parties concerned are on some level aware that this is not very healthy.

The possessor and the person being possessed, although they derive some satisfaction from the relationship, often perceive that it is subtly debilitating to both parties.

My wife is a beautiful woman and I guess I *am* the possessive type. For years I kept tabs on her. She had to tell me what she did, why, and where. Finally one day she said, "Quit treating me like a child. It makes me feel like a little girl, and I want to do things just to show you that I am separate from you and that you don't own me." It took her saying this to wake me up.

The possessive relationship is a tired relationship. To let go of it not only uncomplicates life but increases autonomy, self-reliance, and self-worth—in short, it fosters healthy interdependence.

Devitalized relationships are usually more easily recognized because they offer questionable satisfactions. The bonds of the relationship are tenuous, and there is a recognition that few, if any, common interests or concerns are now shared. A feeling of boredom or surfeit is present, and habit appears to play a major role in maintaining the relationship.

Whenever we get together we talk about the same things. We seem to cover the same ground. The old spark is not there anymore. We've said it all, and it feels as though we are a drag on each other.

A devitalized relationship is exhausting to the participants. It absorbs and drains energy without awareness by the people involved. We need to recognize not only that human relationships have their ebb and flow but that people can grow apart and become increasingly estranged. People do outgrow each other.

A phenomenon related to the devitalized relationship is the *energy vampire relationship*. In this relationship usually one and sometimes both participants seem to draw energy from the other person. Often, following time together, one person feels tired, devitalized, discouraged, and mildly depressed or emerges with a subtly impaired self-image. Conversely, the other person may experience increased vitality as a result of the encounter. Surprisingly, people who are losing energy will sometimes pursue the relationship although aware of the consequences.

During a talk on human potential in Texas, one of this book's authors briefly mentioned the energy vampire relationship. A lady in her mid-forties came up at the end of the lecture and said in an agitated tone of voice:

> I can really believe what you just said about the energy vampire. I have had a friendship with this woman for over twenty years. We see each other every five or six months. She lives over 350 miles away, and she comes to town and stays with me a couple of days. She's bored in the small town she lives in, and her husband doesn't help any. I know I've helped her a lot over the years, and she seems to listen to me when I talk. But she always comes with new problems and difficulties. This has been going on for as long as I can remember, and I always feel drained when she leaves. The last two or three times she has visited I've had to go to bed for a couple of days. After hearing you talk I realize it's been like pouring my energy down a drain.

Another kind of stifling relationship is one based on neurotic needs. Often people seek another person to "complete" themselves, with the unrealistic expectation that somehow if they find the "right one" they will not need to develop certain characteristics for themselves. Some who feel weak and helpless and who lack self-confidence may seek out strong, assertive partners and then count on their strength to get them by. Of course, these decisions are not made deliberately but rather are the result of "unconscious collusion": Two people seek to establish patterns of living together that help them to maintain their views of themselves, others, and the world. Although this style of relating serves the purpose of preserving the comfort of "normalcy," it exacts a toll in personality development.

The price paid for perpetuating *neurotic relationships* is a lopsided life that fails to allow full development of one's potentialities. Neurotic relationships are characterized by rigid patterns that *must* be maintained to keep the needed balance going.

> When I married my husband I needed a strong person to help me feel secure. His needs were met by being able to dominate and control me. As long as I was weak and he was strong we got along just fine. But finally, I got tired of being treated like a child and the whole thing just fell apart.

Obviously, if either partner in a neurotic relationship grows or changes in any way the relationship is in trouble. The alternative, of course, is not to grow and not to develop or utilize all of one's potential. Distorting and limiting oneself in order to maintain a neurotic relationship is both exhausting and unrewarding.

A final type of tired relationship is the *toxic relationship*. Here one person seems to have the unfortunate effect of reawakening or restimulating pathogenic processes, or areas of dysfunctioning or malfunctioning, within the personality of the other. This is sometimes described as "when I am with that person, he/she brings out the worst in me," or "I've noticed that after I am with him/her, I get irritated or depressed and take it out on the people around me."

Often, following a meeting in a toxic relationship, one or both persons may engage in self-destructive behavior, or do things that will hurt others, without being aware of the origins of such actions. Toxic relationships complicate life and reduce its quality.

Sometimes these noxious influences accumulate until their toll can no longer be ignored or tolerated.

Letting Go of Images from Former Relationships

There is a universal tendency to carry into the present the images of former relationships. Many times they continue to exert a strong influence and complicate our lives. Among these potent images are those derived from former relationships to people we adopted as models or idols in our lives: old loves and ex-spouses, mentors, parents. All too often the images of former relationships diminish the quality of experiencing life in the present. They also obscure the unique individual hidden *behind* the image from the past. As one person put it, "I related to the parent of twenty to thirty years ago and never saw the person of today." The process of letting go of the shadows of former tired relationships can bring increased sharing, self-understanding, new perspectives, and new vitality.

A number of class participants decided to each make a list of images from former relationships that they needed to let go. The following is a composite list drawn up by class members with some of their comments and observations.

MENTORS

• I dated this guy and he taught me a lot and helped me a great deal. I thought he knew everything! But then I started to help him and the shoe was on the other foot. He wanted to pull out. I felt like I had to hang on to him. I still see him occasionally, but I can now let him go.

• I used to put this teacher I had in college on a pedestal. I would drop by his office for some very intense discussions. He became more of a person as time passed, but before I could really enjoy him as a friend, I had to let go of the authority image I had carried with me for so many years.

IDOLS AND MODELS

• Our next-door neighbor was my idol. She was perfect as a housekeeper, mother, and in everything else she did. She was my ideal. I used her as a standard, but I could never measure up to her. This class has helped me to see the folly of unrealistic idealizing of relationships. I finally realized what I was doing to myself.

• I really worshipped my first boss and modeled myself after him. I did this for the five years I stayed with the company. He was the kind of guy who would check all the dots on the *i*'s. For three years after I left, I was the same way. Then someone told me I expected too much. It shook me up, and I changed.

CHILDREN

• Children? I thought I owned mine. I even had ideas about their avocations and their careers. I knew what they should do and be. I was hanging on to them tooth and nail. It was the toughest job in my life to give them up and let them go, but the payoff was worth it. We now have a new relationship, infinitely better than the old possessive one.

• I expected my child to be a physician. This would be the third generation of physicians in our family, and that was important to me. He wanted to paint. Even as a small boy he had the talent, but for years I tried to change his mind. An older colleague at the hospital was going through a similar situation. When I saw what it did to his son, it hit me in the solar plexus, and I stopped pressuring. We have been a much happier family since my decision to let up.

FIRST LOVES AND OLD LOVES

• Sometimes I still think about my first love, when I was an early teen. I thought he had all the qualities I wanted. I'm aware that I've romanticized him. He probably was never that way. The other day I met him again for the first time in fifteen years. He was bald and fifty pounds overweight. Who needs this romanticized stuff?

FORMER SPOUSES

• I would wake up at night and hate him. Even after I was happily remarried. It took years. . . .

• I kept watching my second wife, expecting her to turn out like the first. I kept comparing, looking, probing. I finally talked about it to my best friend on an out-of-state trip. He told me I was ruining my marriage and to let go of these comparisons.

PARENTS AND RELATIVES

• I hated my mother—especially as a teenager. This carried over into my marriage. I couldn't even like my husband's mother, although she was completely different from mine. Then I had an experience in a growth group that changed me. I finally let that old image of mothers go. I began to see that Mother had her good points and also her faults like everyone else. For the first time my mother became a real person to me.

• In my mind Dad was a loser. He was an army colonel and a stickler. I was a rebel. We fought continuously. I couldn't let go of Dad, but I finally accepted him for what he is. He now accepts me, and we respect each other and our differences.

• I had this love affair with my aunt from childhood until my mid-twenties. There was no one I liked more, including my family. I always ran to her for advice, and she told me what to do. I became really dependent on her not only for advice but for money and emotional support. On my twenty-sixth birthday I finally declared my independence. I still think she's a love, but

I realized I had to let a lot of those dependencies go if I was ever to grow up and be my own person.

Rejuvenating the Relationship

Sometimes rather than terminating a tired relationship, it may be well to rejuvenate it. There are certain advantages to doing this. The most important ones were summarized by a twenty-seven-year-old professional woman in the course of a group meeting:

> I thought about it, and decided I'd rather not terminate this particular relationship even though it could be classified as a tired one. I decided I'd like to make a try at rebuilding it. There are some positives to this. First, we've known each other for a long time. We respect and like each other, and that's a plus. I believe it's worth saving. We've got something to build on, and I'm willing to make the initial effort.

Rejuvenating a tired relationship depends on the presence of at least four major factors. They are:

1. Mutual regard, liking, or respect. If this is absent in one or both, the outlook is indeed dim.
2. Open communication with emphasis on honesty and caring confrontation in dialogue. This needs to be coupled with a strong desire *not* to use words to hide behind.
3. Willingness to risk and invest effort and energy. At least one person, and preferably both, must be able to give in this manner.
4. Willingness to accept growth and change in oneself and in others.

If you wish to rejuvenate or reconcile a tired relationship you can benefit from obtaining professional help and counseling. Nothing is more discouraging than to risk a reinvolvement and then suffer yet another disappointment. Such hurt can often be avoided by enlisting an objective friend or an expert in communication to guide and mediate such efforts. Your renewal efforts are unlikely to succeed without new insights and approaches, and these changes are more likely to occur with professional help.

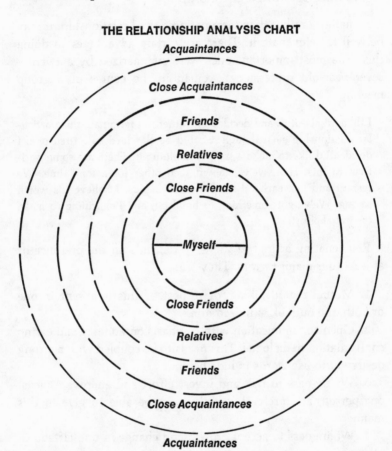

THE RELATIONSHIP ANALYSIS CHART

Acquaintances

Close Acquaintances

Friends

Relatives

Close Friends

Myself

Close Friends

Relatives

Friends

Close Acquaintances

Acquaintances

Relationship Analysis

An excellent basic step in the direction of uncomplicating life consists of an analysis of your relationships. This is sometimes called the *relationship field.* Most people have never taken a clear look at the range and nature of their relationships with people. Very often what they discover comes as a considerable surprise. One class member on completing the relationship analysis commented, "I never realized I had this imbalance in my relationships until I filled out this chart. It was a shock." Another participant reported:

> When I did the quality analysis part of the relationship analysis I discovered that I had surrounded myself with neutral or toxic people. This explained a lot of things that had puzzled me, and I made up my mind to turn the whole thing around.

The Relationship Analysis Chart contains a series of concentric circles in which to write the names of close friends, relatives, and acquaintances. Begin the analysis by writing your name in the center of the small circle in the middle of the chart. Next, fill in as many names in the various concentric circles as you can. After you have filled in the chart, put it aside for a period of time, or better still, until the next day. Then look the chart over and add any names to the list you may have left out.

Quality Analysis

At this point you are ready for the second part of your relationship analysis—the *quality analysis*. Look over the names on your chart in the light of the following two questions:

1. What people make me feel good; increase my self-esteem; stimulate me; bring out my creativity; help me be more spontaneous or witty; or make me laugh more and enjoy life and myself more? (*nurturant people*)

2. What people have a neutral to negative effect on me; bore me; make me question my self-worth; make me feel "blue," anxious, depressed or angry; have rigid expectations; accept only certain parts of me; or leave me feeling frustrated or drained? (*toxic people*)

3. What people neither add to or detract from my life? (*neutral people*)

As you look over your chart keep the above questions in mind. Identify the nurturant people by putting a plus mark beside their names. Mark out the toxic people with an X. Designate those who are neither nurturant or toxic with a big zero—since that is what they add to your life.

What kind of people do you find in your chart? Remember that the people you marked with an X are *tired relationships*. You can uncomplicate your life and gain a sense of exhilarating freedom by letting go of such relationships. How many neutral people can you allow to drain your life's energy? Do you have an adequate number of strong affirming voices to make it all worthwhile?

Kim R. filled out the Relationship Analysis form in class and commented:

> I never realized I was involved with so many neutral people. I found it very interesting to look at the people I know in this way. I have a few toxic and a few nurturant ones. I would guess a couple more are borderline toxic, but I am giving them the benefit of the doubt. My discovery is that I need more nurturant people in my life!

Another type of relationship analysis consists of an examination of the aims and purposes involved in specific social relationships. This type of analysis is not as effective or comprehensive and is usually limited to selected and relatively few persons. Although most people find themselves resistant to undertaking such an analysis, the results are often illuminating. The key question to be asked is, "What do I get out of a specific relationship?"

Henry G. analyzed his social relationships as follows:

Jim—mostly business.
Harold—like him, would like to know better.
The Kellys—challenging, stimulating, controversial ideas.

Sam and Helen R.—bores, and indifferent.

Donald K.—could be a friend. I've neglected him. He helps me grow.

After completing the above analysis, Henry B. commented:

At first I did not want to ask myself that question, but I did it anyway and learned a great deal. For example, I like the Kellys but have put off seeing them because they challenged some of my ideas. Their style made me uncomfortable, but I realize I need this influence in my life and I am going to see more of them. I have also made up my mind to try and have a friendship with Donald. The relationship with Sam and Helen has nothing to offer, and I decided after this analysis to end it.

Emily H., a young unmarried career woman, found some surprises when she did her own personal relationship analysis:

Susan—Now a "duty" relationship based on past commitments. Not personally pleasurable. We've changed in different directions over the years.

Emily—Fun! Exhilarating! Challenges me to do new things.

Jane—I see her out of responsibility. She leans on me. It's a superficial but neutral relationship. She adds nothing to my life. It's status quo.

Jack—Comfortable to be with. I like to be with him.

Andy—He uses me. I feel on guard when we're together—just waiting for the next "barb."

From the above exercise Emily found that one of her best friends was soon to become a former friend and that her current steady boyfriend lost out to a man she had failed to give any serious attention to in the past. She also clarified some new relationships with a number of her women friends and became more aware of some things she hoped could happen in her relationships with the others.

Letting Go of Tired Relationships Isn't Always Easy

Ending a tired relationship with a person you have known for some time doesn't always bring immediate exhilaration. To expect that response is unrealistic. Even harmful and disappointing relationships are difficult to lose when we have become accustomed to them. Be prepared instead for some "separation anxiety" and even a period of mourning. One class member described how she had reacted. She was so depressed that she became physically ill for four months:

> Even though I intellectually understood that ending the relationship was my only hope for health and self-esteem, I just couldn't get myself moving. I lost all interest in life and found myself barely able to handle my job. Hearing a romantic song on the radio would start the tears flowing, and no amount of head tripping helped. I felt like I was down at the bottom and would never feel joy again.

"Down" is an acceptable place to be temporarily, and it is more likely to be temporary if you face the loss openly and allow yourself really to feel it. *Don't deny your feelings.* It is only by working them through that you can resolve them. All reconstruction work is not painless. It is necessary to accept temporary pain in order to avoid chronic pain.

"Moment of Truth"

Clark Moustakas in his book *Individuality and Encounter* has this to say about relationships:

> In our meetings with others, conflicts arise and feelings of irritation grow until we no longer can continue to live with each other in the same way. Thus, either the relationship will continue to deteriorate or the people will face each other and struggle with the issues and the problems. . . . It is a private, intimate conflict between people which happens, often spontaneously and unexpectedly, when a crisis arises in a relationship and [those concerned] must

either reach a new level of life together or face the consequences of a broken relationship, evasiveness, distortion and alienation. (Moustakas 1968, p. 53).

One key question is: "Which is most painful: to end a tired relationship, or to deceive oneself into believing that it still has meaning, and that loyalty, or habit, or fear is worth more than honesty and the courage to say good-bye?" Most people are aware that it is difficult to end a tired relationship, but they often fail to realize the high price they pay when they fail to let it go. It is much like the struggle a person goes through in thinking about divorce. Often the fear of getting out of the marriage is linked to a clear realization that change in one's life will not be easy. We can usually see the problems inherent in letting go, but what we often fail to see is the high price we pay by staying in a destructive relationship.

People faced with a decision of whether or not to end a relationship will find it useful to ask the above key question. Each answer must be unique, influenced by numerous, complex feelings and factors. These decisions generally encompass two broad areas: (1) doubts about whether one has the right to end a relationship that may still seem to have validity for the partner; and (2) the fear of the actual *process* of terminating. Here the following series of questions can be useful:

1. Would you still try to develop a relationship if you met for the first time today?
2. Does the relationship enhance or diminish you?
3. What are *you* getting from the relationship?
4. How do you feel about the relationship *now*?
5. Are you being honest with yourself about this relationship or are you deceiving yourself?
6. Is a misplaced loyalty, habit, or fear of social stigma keeping you from ending the relationship?
7. Do you have the courage to say good-bye?
8. Is the relationship worth rejuvenating?

Ways to End Relationships

Often a reluctance to make a conscious decision to end a relationship makes people prefer to "drift along" until one day they discover, often with surprise, that through neglect a relationship has ended anyway and their passivity has forfeited their options.

> I knew we should confront some issues and have a heart-to-heart talk, but we kept putting it off. I guess I was the timid one and was most responsible for the postponed meetings. Finally it was too late. The damage had been done, and we both realized the relationship was over. The tragedy is we might have repaired it earlier—or at least we could have ended it in a less hurtful way.

We cannot simply maintain a status quo. We can face issues and settle problems. Or we can face the fact that the relationship will probably deteriorate, and be forced to let it go or to "make do" with what is left.

A number of options exist for those who make a decision to end a relationship. The most popular of these is the *time as terminator* process. This consists of a gradual withdrawal from the relationship with the verbal and/or written contact diminishing over a period of time until all contact ceases. The other person senses what is taking place and cooperates in the process. This avoids confrontation, and the reasons for the termination of the relationship do not have to be explicitly made. Many times one person in this process does not know why the relationship is being terminated.

The *gentle parting* is the second most popular way of ending a relationship. There is either a last personal meeting or phone conversation. During this exchange a reason or a strong hint for terminating the relationship may be given. Confrontations are avoided and emphasis is on making the parting as painless as possible.

The *written way of termination* is less often used. In a note or lengthy letter reasons for termination are given. Further contact is avoided. One class member shared the following note:

> Dear Paula:
> I have noticed we have been seeing each other less and less over the past year. When we do meet we usually have very little to say to each other. Our worlds and interests have changed, and we seem to be miles apart. I am sure you will recall that we touched on this at our last luncheon. I shall always treasure our earlier friendship and wish you the best.

Confrontation as a final clearing is the least popular mode of ending a relationship. This usually consists of a face-to-face meeting to discuss causes and share feelings related to the termination. The objective is to clear the air once and for all. The danger of this process is that it may end in a hostile or hurtful exchange which can wound one or both persons. Unfortunately, knowing how to "confront" is a skill that few people have. It includes the ability to face an issue squarely and still be supportive and open to the other's perceptions:

> We had this final meeting and I went through all the feelings that led up to it. I really got my feelings out. This caused an explosion, and I guess we both felt we had been kicked in the teeth. What a way to end a friendship after six years of knowing and caring about each other.

Constructive confrontation, however, is a very productive way to maintain personal integrity and still reinforce meaningful interpersonal exchange that can clarify a relationship. It is not destructive or hostile and its purpose is to create a discussion in which issues can be dealt with honestly and realistically.

> Personal honesty is very important to me, and I wanted to talk about it. This led to both of us being completely honest and open with each other. On our last meeting our emotions just spilled over. We screamed and then cried a little. Finally we both agreed our values had changed since we first became friends. I think we both grew a little through this final meeting. It was a good ending.

Courage, risk taking, openness, and sensitivity are important if the confrontation process is used as a means of termination. Skillfully handled, confrontation as a final clearing can yield gains in self-confidence and self-worth for both people.

A Planned Termination

Sometimes it is necessary to end a relationship with someone who has become really dependent upon you. You may be aware that this person does not have many other friends. When ending a relationship in these circumstances, do some actual *planning* so that the process will not be an unduly traumatic or uncomfortable one for either of you. Such a planned termination may take four or five weeks to accomplish and can predictably involve several "stages," such as denial; expressions of need, sadness, and loss; hostility or depression; acceptance and resolution. Your responsiveness to the other person and the way you handle this process will have a great deal to do with how quickly your friend will recover emotionally after you "let go."

Such a planned termination begins by explicit statements of your intent to end the relationship by a certain date—three or four weeks in the future. You could meet or talk with the person several times in the interim, reinforcing that intention and helping him or her deal with the feelings associated with your letting go. To end a relationship this thoughtfully can be a most important evidence of caring since, by doing so, you will minimize the feelings of rejection that the other will develop. A class member commented:

> I was on the receiving end of a breakup. I had been very dependent on that person and she told me she gradually wanted to withdraw from our relationship. This gave me time to adjust and work on my feelings. We met several more times. Then I saw clearly that we had developed different interests. On our last meeting I told her she had been very thoughtful.

When tired relationships are maintained only out of a sense of duty, it exacts a toll, not only of time, but also of mental and physical health. Discontinuing tired relationships frees time to meet interesting new people. Finally, guilt about a "neglected relationship" is eliminated. A conscious decision to drop certain people from your list of social acquaintances, or relationships, can bring new vitality and energy to you and to your social life.

CHAPTER 4

Letting Go
of the Past

ONE DAY I was standing in line at a campus restaurant to pay my
lunch bill when I noticed an older man shuffle toward the cash
register. I recognized him immediately. Fifteen years ago he had
been president of the university and for more than two decades
had guided it with skill through some of its greatest years of
growth. He asked the cashier for some direction and then started
to turn away as if to go. He hesitated and then turned to the
young lady at the register and said, "You don't know me, do
you? I am the man for whom this building was named." With
those words he turned again and moved slowly down the hall.
His era was over, that was poignantly clear. There was no way
for him to recapture the past.

I inquired and learned that upon retirement the university had
given this past president a complimentary office in a nearby
building. Every morning he drove to the university, but there
was no work for him to do. No one asked his advice or called
his office, but he never failed to come. He spent his days wandering about the institution reminding people that he had once been
its president.

Too many of us spend our energy thinking about the past and
dwelling on how things used to be. Our minds become dulled by
our constant preoccupation with events that are already history;

we carry with us the dead weight of issues and concerns about past experiences. But these experiences are over; they can't be changed. They need to be put aside and forgotten. All they can do is block our best thinking and rob us of energy that might be used productively to deal with present experiences, over which we could exert some control if we were able to approach each day with our full measure of energy.

Letting Go of the Past as a Process of Growth

Personality is a process. Life and events are a process. If we fail to move with these processes we may find ourselves behaving in irrelevant and nonproductive ways. Life is not static; it is dynamic. To live means to outlive. To grow is to outgrow and to let go. Ideas, behaviors, values, friends, and other facets of our lives that were useful at one stage may very well become a burden at another. Winfred Rhoades, in *Have You Lost God?*, observed, "Growing is outgrowing and very often this kind of growth can come only as the fruit of pain."

All around us are reminders that this is so. The lobster is a good example. Its growth depends on the shedding of a series of hard, protective shells. The shell that protected and served it well at one stage eventually becomes too small for its expanding body. If the shell cannot be dropped as the lobster expands, it will smother and kill the fish. But letting go of the shell is also a risk. When the hard, protective cover is gone, for a time the lobster is left soft, pliable, and vulnerable to attack. It is only in this soft and pliable state that it can create a new and expanded shell that allows for continued growth.

The apostle Paul referred to this process when he said, "When I was a child I spake as a child; when I grew up I put away childish things."

How does one put away childish things and move into adulthood? It is not an easy task, and it is clear that some people never accomplish it. They fail to feel the pull of the future, and childish things seem to serve them well all their lives. Dr. J.

Paterson Smyth, a noted theologian, made a cogent observation in this regard:

> There are many good people to whom the notions learned at a
> Christian mother's knee are very dear and sufficiently true for the
> guidance of life—many who claim absolute knowledge of truth and
> to whom newer views would be but a source of disturbance. It is
> perhaps not needful for them to inquire any further. Let them rest
> in peace feeding on God's green pastures beside His still waters. But
> let them remember that it is not given to all people thus to rest,
> that restlessness as well as rest may be a gift of God, His path to a
> higher knowledge of truth.
>
> (Smyth, *How God Inspired the Bible*)

Although some fail to recognize that many of their childhood concepts are not adequate for later life, others do feel the need to move on, to grow. They replace outworn ideas and attitudes with new ones that are more relevant and helpful in meeting the complexities of adult living. The process of moving on requires effort, but there are benefits for engaging in the task.

Expanding Your Awareness, the Initial Step

The first step in letting go of childish things begins with an awareness that you would like to make some changes in your life. Your life is not as fulfilling as it could be; it may be boring at times. There may be a lack of vitality in your experiences. You may recognize that the routine style of your existence has caused your life to lose its excitement. Until you become aware of such feelings, you probably won't seek any change. You will simply go along wondering what has robbed you of your energy and assume that life is dull and difficult for everyone.

Awareness is usually sparked by unique experience, or perhaps by meeting a new friend. Suddenly you realize that it has been a long time since you've felt such zest and excitement. Meeting a stimulating acquaintance reinforces the difference between what life is for you and what it seems to be for the person you have just met. You wonder about the discrepancy. You begin to catalogue some of the changes that could make a difference in your own life. *Such an awareness can bring a new beginning.* A middle-aged housewife describes one of her awareness-enhancing experiences in these words:

> It had been years since I'd seen Barbara. What a difference! I just couldn't get over how she had changed from a semiattractive, rather common-looking person into a vibrant and totally fascinating woman. As she described her current interests and activities, I found myself comparing my sense of boredom and resignation to her enthusiasm and obvious anticipation and my inertia to her apparent capacity to develop new interests and to take her life off into all kinds of new directions. It was a shock to realize how she had grown and expanded while I had just been drifting along, never looking to the right or to the left.

Making a Decision

Once aware of which changes you want to make in your life, you will have to decide whether or not you will follow through. This must be a conscious decision on your part, one that carries with it a commitment of energy to bring about the shifts you desire. A plaque hanging above the door in an old southern church clearly states why a conscious decision is necessary: "Not to decide is to decide."

Often the status quo is more comfortable than change, and we simply adapt our life to whatever is least disconcerting. It is frightening to see how easily we can adjust to almost anything. We need to understand how we accumulate our emotional overloads from the past. To add one more worry, one more concern, or one more mistake to the problems we are already carrying may not seem like much at the time. The accretion is so slow that we fail to realize how heavy our load is becoming and how carrying it robs us of energy we could use in other activities. We get bogged down with the weight of our accumulating burdens, never realizing how much of the past we are dragging with us into the future. If we are to reclaim our energy, we must unload the useless, unproductive baggage of the past.

Sorting the Wheat from the Chaff

Another step in letting go of the past is to do some sorting. There are good memories, experiences, lessons, relationships, and mementos that give roots to your life and continually support your growth and sense of well-being. It is important to be able to distinguish between these positive elements of one's past and those that have had a negative effect on your emotional growth. Too often destructive experiences, or mistakes, are given power in your present life because of the time you spend reliving them. You revive again and again your losses, your disappointments, and your feelings of rejection.

You may also worry not simply about mistakes but about past events that can't be changed. You wonder if you should have behaved differently on some specific occasions. You fret about things you wish you had done and also about things you wish you had not done. You spend precious energy remembering past conversations and rehearsing verbal exchanges that will probably never occur. You agonize about relationships that are no longer viable and replay roles that are no longer possible or useful. You continually involve yourself in fruitless search for reasons why this or that happened.

Stephanie had been married for seventeen years, yet she still played old records from her high school days and tried to figure out why she had married Blaine instead of Steve. How could the junior prom queen possibly have ended up in such a routine existence? Every day seemed the same. Blaine was up early and off to work at an insurance company that held little opportunity for advancement. Her job each day was to get the four children ready for school and then take care of the house and be sure that things were in order when the group returned for dinner at night. Blaine was usually tired and television seemed to meet his needs for the evening. It was a drab existence. At this stage college sounded exciting, and she kept wondering why she hadn't gone to Purdue with Steve.

It went on and on. Every day was filled with rehearsing past mistakes and endless "What ifs" for Stephanie. This only robbed her of energy that might have been better spent on trying to deal with her life in the present.

The time comes when you must sort out unproductive behavior and move on. You may have made some mistakes. You may have hurt yourself or others, but, if you cannot do something constructive about whatever continues to plague your thoughts and frustrate your days, you need to put their memory aside.

Getting Rid of Past Baggage

One way to begin the sorting process is to use the Baggage from the Past Chart that appears here. Write down the attitudes and behavior patterns you want to discard. Keep paper available so you can add to your list whenever you become aware of additional baggage that weighs you down. Once you have identified your problem areas, your actions can more purposefully eradicate the useless attitudes and behavior that have been robbing you of energy.

Many other examples could be added to the list of baggage described on the left-hand side of the chart. Write down your excess baggage in the column at your right. If necessary, use extra sheets of paper. As you make your own list, you may become aware of the attitudes and behaviors you continue to carry with you even though they have no role to play in your life. Note what your feelings are *as you write*. Analyze your list and begin the process of letting go. Maybe you will feel some anger as you become aware of the loads you have been carrying. You can express this anger—by pounding a pillow, yelling, etc. Say to yourself, "I've got to get it out of my system!" Repeat the process until you do.

BAGGAGE FROM THE PAST CHART

Type of Baggage	Baggage That You Need to Let Go
1. Reliving your mistakes	
2. Harboring bad things people have done to you	
3. Harboring bad things you have done to others	
4. Brooding on events that can't be changed	
5. Worrying about your behavior long after specific occasions	
6. Fretting about things you wish you had done and others you wish you had not done	
7. Rehearsing conversations with people that will probably never happen	
8. Planning ways to respond to things that will probably never occur	
9. Reliving your losses	
10. Wishing for things that are unrealistic	
11. Agonizing about relationships that are no longer a part of your life	

12. Playing roles that are no longer possible, useful, or appropriate

13. Continuing to wish that things were different

14. Involving yourself in a fruitless search for reasons "why"

15. Wondering why certain things happened to you

16. Others

Companies all over the country are beginning to realize the value of creating special exercise rooms where employees can work off excess energy and rid themselves of emotional overloads by *physical exercises*. One company in Chicago provided a special room where men and women who felt the need to unload anger and frustration could go and sling dishes at a brick wall for as long as they felt the need.

Oftentimes there are emotional triggers in the environment that set off memories, feelings, or associations connected with baggage from the past. Such triggers may be mementos, keepsakes, art, photographs, records, certain pieces of furniture, or even the arrangement of furniture.

Take a piece of paper and go from room to room analyzing your environment for such emotional triggers. Do these triggers sap your energy and make you think too much about the past? Eliminate as many of these triggers as you can.

Trusting Yourself

Another approach in letting go of the past is to seek help from others. Gather all the information and suggestions you can and then use the good ideas to help you make your own decisions.

It is, however, important to remember that if you are to keep control of what happens for you and to you, you will ultimately need to take personal responsibility for your choices. Having a collection of good ideas can be of great assistance, but when final decisions are made you must be willing to trust yourself to choose from the available alternatives. No one is in as good a position as you to determine what it is you want and need.

Unfortunately, it is not always easy to trust ourselves and to believe that we know better than anyone what is best for us. So much in our culture robs us of our confidence and suggests that we should turn to outside authorities for answers to our dilemmas. From an early age other people have made decisions for us and about us. Often they have not even involved us in the process, and this, in part, is why we have never learned how to make decisions for ourselves.

As a result of having had little experience in decision making, some of us have developed few skills at sorting out the pros and cons of issues. If we have limited skills, we have difficulty trusting ourselves to make a decision. If we have difficulty trusting ourselves in making a decision, we develop few skills. It is a vicious cycle that reinforces itself.

Margaret wanted a new look in her home. It seemed as if everything had worn out at the same time, and she decided to splurge on new carpets, furniture, accessories. Everything needed to be changed! Of course, with such a major undertaking at hand, she knew she'd *have* to get an interior decorator. When he suggested colors or fabrics she didn't like, she didn't dare say no. After all, *he* was an expert, and his bill proved it! Many weeks and thousands of dollars later, when she was stuck with a room that made her sick, she confided to a friend that she felt as though she had been mentally raped and had been powerless against the persuasion of the "expert" she had hired.

If you get caught a few times in this kind of an "expert" trap and it begins to hurt, you may decide to risk making some decisions for yourself. Decision making is a skill and like most skills must be learned. Only if you jump in and begin to test your abilities will you discover what you can and cannot do.

This is not easy, but neither is it easy to stay caught in a trap. The big advantage to risking and trying something new is that you might find that you have more skills than you thought.

If you find that you have more skills than you had supposed, you will begin to have more successes, and each new success will reinforce your confidence in your ability to make sound decisions. Your sense of confidence will grow as you begin to assume responsibility for determining the pattern of your life. Remember that this process will not be easy, so you must guard against getting discouraged if you don't make "perfect" decisions every time. Skills are not inherited; they do not come automatically. You must concentrate on developing them. You can do this only if you are willing to risk and to learn from your own experiences what works and what does not.

Learning to trust our own sense of things is often a long and difficult process. We are conditioned and programmed to respond the way others think we should respond. Whenever we question group norms or operate outside our assigned role or status, there is always someone hanging around to challenge our right to make such a decision. Do you ever ask, "What makes me think I am smart enough to make a decision for myself?" particularly when you do not agree with the decision of some proclaimed outside authority.

The spirit of owning and taking control of one's own life rings loud and clear in these diary entries:

> Yes, I am changing directions. I am determined not to operate within a role or a status. I do not want to allow a role to define me, to render me helpless, trapped, uncomfortable. Rather, now *I* will define myself and breathe life into that role, knowing my own sense of self in it all.
>
> The critical thing, I guess, is trusting the process that's going on inside me. Listening to it, moving with it, not questioning. I am willing to let the past go. I will not get stuck in limits that I've assumed or set limits on my possibilities. I will make no demands on what must stay and what must go. I will just let go and move on when it feels right to move.

Handling Past Traumas

All of us will inevitably have some pain or traumatic experiences in our lives. This is unavoidably a part of living. But, even though we cannot prevent such experiences, we do have the power to determine whether they will hurt us just once, or *many* times. If we continue to reenact in memory a past pain, we give the person or the event that caused the pain in the first place the power to hurt us over and over again. We can make the choice: We can leave ourselves vulnerable. Or we can decide to take control of what has occurred in the past.

We might learn a useful survival technique from observing the design of the modern submarine. When a portion of a submarine becomes damaged, it is designed so that the affected area can be sealed off in a watertight compartment, thus preventing the escape of damaging seawater into other areas of the ship. To avoid the spread of a damaging or poisoning memory of the past it is sometimes possible to learn all we can from the traumatic experience and then seal it off in a memory-tight compartment.

Sometimes, however, it is not possible to handle a past trauma by sealing it off or by dismissing it. Sometimes hurtful memories must be symbolically relived or reexperienced in an emotional "instant replay" that will help us to resolve them in a positive, cleansing way. At times a trusted friend can help us to heal our past wounds just by listening to our story and helping us explore all of its causes and effects, while offering us the understanding and support that were so lacking in the original experience.

When there is pain too difficult to share with another, we can find relief in various "do-it-yourself" ways. For some it is helpful to write down the experience, embellishing each detail until all of the psychological infection is cleansed from the emotional wound.

Others find it helpful to draw pictures and throw darts at them, to hit symbols of a hated person or event with a rolled newspaper while shouting out accumulated anger and hostility, or to use punching bags or a brick wall. Some can work out their rage and anger on the tennis court or jogging, playing a musical instrument, or attacking a hard physical task. The important thing about working through past traumas is to get in touch with your feelings, to own and accept them as they are, and to consciously tell yourself that you are releasing pain and poison from your life through whatever activity works for you.

Sometimes experiences that are traumatic at the moment can become a family joke. Ruth recounted such an occasion in one of her classes:

My pastor asked if I would say a closing prayer at our meeting the following week. It seemed like a simple enough assignment, so I agreed. I wanted to do an exceptionally good job, so I went home and committed my prayer to memory. On Sunday when he called on me I felt confident enough until I forgot the fourth line. At that point I panicked and simply sat down, failing to finish the prayer. Afterwards I was hopelessly embarrassed and for weeks could not return to the assembly. I lived and relived the experience.

One day a group from the church visited me. They didn't dodge the issue at all. They brought up the incident in a good-humored way and shared some of *their* embarrassing moments with me. We all had a good laugh, and it became obvious to me that everyone has their "traumatic" experiences and no one but me was worrying about mine.

I learned a couple of things from that experience. First, I learned that good humor can turn some of our traumas into trivia, and secondly, I learned never to memorize my prayers.

If old wounds fail to heal, you may need to enlist the help of a professional person. Sally had a fine job and was now 3,000 miles away from her tyrannical father, but she was still immobilized by an irrational fear that haunted her each time she thought of home and her parents. The fear robbed her of energy and was responsible for the high incidence of illness that appeared in her work record. This fear, realistic and appropriate when she was a dependent, powerless, threatened little girl, was highly inappropriate under the present circumstances; but try as she did, she could not let it go. Only with therapeutic help was she able at last to leave her pain where it belonged—in her past.

Maude talked excitedly about the new freedom she'd found since going to a marriage counselor:

> I really didn't think anyone could help me get over the nagging pain that's been around my heart since John walked out on me nearly a year ago. His going was such a loss. I really didn't want to give up believing he'd come back and I hated to bury the memories we'd shared even though remembering nearly killed me. It took nearly nine months for me to become convinced that I needed to let go of all the garbage that was cluttering my life and dulling my enthusiasm for living.
>
> It was hard to make the decision to go for professional help, but now I'm glad I did. I've dropped all the heavy weights that pulled me down and that nagging pain around my heart is finally gone.

Letting Go of Useless Traditions

Some of the traditions we inherit from the past are priceless and add luster to our lives. Others are simply traditions that, having served another generation well, are honored, preserved, and passed on in a loving and irrational way with the assumption that they will also serve the present generation.

This is not always a safe assumption. Like so many things in our lives, traditions need sifting and sorting. Too often we hang on to them simply because they are defined as traditions. We feel bound to preserve them whether we like them or not, and feel a sense of guilt even after we have evaluated them and decided to let them go. Like so many things, letting go of useless traditions begins with recognizing them. One young man expressed it this way:

> Before I left home I felt hidebound and structured in so many ways, I didn't think I'd ever free myself from all the imposed entanglements. I not only didn't think I'd ever be free but I thought I'd never want to go back home again. My memory of that place was so

cluttered with all the things we *had* to do just because we were Randalls. We had traditions running out our ears. It's hard to believe any family would hang on to so many behaviors that simply had to happen just because grandpa and grandma thought they were important seventy years ago.

They may have worked for them and they even seem to be working for some members of the family, but they certainly don't all work for me. Getting away was good for me. I'm surprised to find that I'm beginning to miss some of them. I never thought I would, but I was wrong. I think I just needed a chance to let go of everything and some time to figure out which traditions made sense to me and which did not. I'm ready now to reclaim some of them.

It's funny how differently I feel about them now that I've freely chosen some of them for myself. I've learned that being rooted is good but being rootbound is crippling. I feel like I'm involved in a whole new process. I've shed everything and now I'm ready to pick and choose and reclaim only those things I really want to claim.

Perhaps no better example of how traditions get started and supported for irrational reasons is the story a fifty-nine-year-old woman told the people in her cooking class one evening as they began the lesson of preparing pineapple ham for a festive occasion:

You won't believe it, but for ten years I cut ham into small pieces and basted it with pineapple juice. Grandma always did hers that way and I figured that was just how you did it. One day I noticed she had cooked it whole and was slicing it for dinner. I was surprised that she'd changed her special recipe and was doing it like everyone else. She just laughed and said, "There was nothing special about my style; I just didn't have a bigger pan."

Traditions, like behaviors, can become excess baggage. They can weigh us down with shoulds and oughts and bind us to directives that make no sense for our own preferred life-style. If we feel bound to honor them and observe them despite their lack of value to us, we can easily find ourselves feeling first dependent and then hostile.

Sometimes we need to be rescued from our traditions. We need to stand back and take a hard look, far enough back so that the sun can get in between the cracks and shed some light on the possibilities that are available. With some illumination and perspective we can perhaps make better choices about which traditions we will honor and which ones we want to let go.

Replacing Discarded Experiences with New Ones

As you begin discarding baggage from the past you will have a revival of energy that can be used to develop new interests and new friendships. This is a good time to experiment a bit. Try some new life-styles. Develop a different approach to old problems. Be creative with your spare time. Now is the time to open yourself to new ideas, visit new places, and attack projects you've always wanted to try but couldn't find the energy. When you let go of the useless baggage you've been carrying and begin to travel lighter, you'll be surprised at how easily you can move and how much freer and more responsive you will feel and act. Not only will you be able to sample many more things in your world but you will have time to experience them in greater depth. You will rediscover people and activities that have been important to you in the past but have been ignored because you couldn't find the time or because it took too much effort.

Describing Yourself with Old Labels

Labeling yourself can be a barrier to growth. It can chain you to a past that will not let you go. Examples of some of the more common labels that we hear everyday are: "I did that because that's the way I am"; "I always do that"; "I never do that"; "I can't help it, I'm just that way"; "I'm sorry, that's just my nature."

To the extent that you accept these labels and get a set image of yourself, you run the risk of becoming a rigid, predictable person who will not allow new experiences to change you or help you grow. Your preconceived notions of who you are and what you can do will determine what you will screen out of your life and what you will let in. You will not expect to change and thus you will continue to act in the future just as you have acted in the past. Such an approach puts into play all the dynamics of a self-fulfilling prophecy. If you continue to label yourself in certain ways you will end up being what you had predicted you would be.

The labels we pin on ourselves or allow to be pinned on us by others are not easy to change. We become habituated to them and usually don't take the time even to wonder where they came from or why they are used to describe us. We simply accept them and go on day after day responding unconsciously to descriptions that structure and restructure us into certain pre-scribed roles.

It's not easy for any of us to deal with the labels in our lives but, if we're ever going to change the patterns they create, we have to start somewhere. Trying to sort out how the labels got started can be instructive. Are we really like that—or are the descriptions irrational ones that were applied to us either in fun or by someone who really didn't know what we're like or what we might become?

Try making a list of all the labels that have been used to describe you.

—Where did they come from?

—Who started them?

—How many do you feel really fit you now?

—Which do you wish you could erase?

—Do any of these labels prevent you from doing things you want to do?

—Say each label aloud, and concentrate on how you feel about each.

—Now, make some decisions about which labels you need to *let go.*

Believing that You Have Some Control over Your Past and Exercising It

If you believe you are simply a victim of your past experiences, you will not believe that you have the power to put them behind you and gain control over your present circumstances. You will simply succumb to the pain and rationalize that you can't do anything about it. You'll blame Mother's rejection or Father's disapproving behavior for any problems you presently have and sit by waiting for sympathy or therapeutic descriptions that will relieve you of personal responsibility. If you find such support you may rationalize your part in the problem, but the rationalization will not relieve the pain. You will be the one to suffer, regardless of who created the problems, so the sooner you convince yourself that you have some control over your life, the sooner you will begin to take over and find the power to solve your own problems.

Your attitude will be the most important ingredient in changing the control you have over the past. When you begin to feel you can be in charge, you will be. You will begin to take over and to determine what you will keep from the past and what you will let go. You will work to destroy self-defeating behaviors and to build confidence in your ability to decide what your life can be.

An individual's past experiences, for all their importance in creating the present difficulties, are not insurmountable barriers. Jim, a recovered alcoholic, described some of his own experiences in these words:

> For years I blamed my present behaviors and conflicts on the fact that my parents were alcoholics and seldom gave much time or attention to me. It was an easy out. Whenever I got into trouble I would simply recount my stormy past as the excuse. Most people bought into my teary tale and could understand why I was like I was. Their understanding reinforced my fears and made it easy for me to remain the same. I spent nearly half my life rationalizing and absorbing sympathy.

I finally realized that no amount of sympathy or understanding could solve my problems or ease my pain. I got tired of hurting all the time. I decided it really didn't matter *who* caused it. I was the one who was hurting, and I learned that I could do something about the problem even if I didn't create it.

Unfortunately, clinging to the past does become a way of life for many, but a high price is paid for this fear-ridden approach to life. When few risks are taken there are few rewards. But most of all, living in the past robs us of the energy to live fully in the present. We spend so much of our time and energy looking backward at closed doors that we fail to see the new doors opening to us every day.

CHAPTER 5

Letting Go
of Security Blankets

MOST OF US HAVE "SECURITY BLANKETS" of one kind or another. Some have served us well for so many years that they have become a part of our life-style. Over the years we have experienced support and comfort from them and often do not recognize that a security blanket that served us legitimately and well at one time in our lives can at a later time become a burden and block our growth rather than support it.

A child hanging on to its bottle at the age of twelve months may well find comfort and security in having its nourishment close at hand; but should the same child take its bottle to school at age six, the comfort and security would probably be replaced by embarrassment and ridicule. At twelve months the bottle would be seen as an appropriate security blanket; at six years it would be a clear announcement of immaturity and lack of growth.

Too often we hold on to inappropriate security blankets which slow us down and prevent our reaching out to new experiences. We accept the ridicule and embarrassment that results from hanging on to them because the idea of letting them go provokes too much anxiety. Often they are so much a part of our behavior patterns that we hang on unconsciously and fail to relate the negative responses to our inappropriate style of behaving.

When Alice told the story of her five-year marriage, she told it with teary eyes and trembling hands. Her husband had had three affairs in those five years and had recently been drinking too much and was abusing her physically. She had lost twenty pounds that she could ill afford and was continually experiencing anxiety and related health problems. At twenty-eight she felt she was a total failure, unlovable, ugly, and boring. She was also convinced that her two young children were suffering irreparable harm because of her marital situation. Her life seemed hopelessly dead-ended. When asked what options she had, besides remaining in such a painful situation, she was silent. It had never occurred to her that she had any other alternative than to stay. She had continued to cling to her husband despite his serious problems. He was her security blanket. She remained with him because she felt it was easier to live with her present pain than to risk the possibility that a change might bring even more discomfort.

What Is a Security Blanket?

A security blanket can be an attitude or a person, place, or thing that has become an inordinate, irrational need and that must be present if a person is to feel secure, important, and cared about. When or if the security blanket should be removed, this person would feel totally lost. Have you ever observed a child who has lost his or her "binkie"—or a grown person who cannot function if the spouse goes out of town?

The outstanding characteristic of a true security blanket is its familiarity. You can always count on it. It is always there. All it asks is that you never discard it and certainly never change, or grow, or rethink certain childhood convictions. In return for giving up freedom, you get security. Some people believe this is not too big a price to pay.

My job offers me financial security, status in the community, a beautiful office, and no small sense of power. In exchange for maintaining such a position I now realize I have given up my own ideas, my sense of ethical justice, and have put tight curbs on my sense of spontaneity. After five years of this emotional hypocrisy, I decided that the price of that kind of "security" was too much to pay.

Security Blankets of Adulthood

Despite their prevalence, the security blankets of adulthood often go unrecognized by the very people who cling to them. These adult security blankets are usually attitudes or things that yield a certain measure of comfort and seemingly help maintain emotional balance. Few grown men and women still cling to actual blankets or bottles, but many adult-type security blankets can be identified. Some of the sources of security used by adults are family name, personal possessions, friends, money, recognition, husband's or wife's position, clothes, church or professional memberships, home, personal talents, influential acquaintances, physical attractiveness, sex, degrees, and honors.

Sometimes inheritances like land, a family business, or priceless heirlooms are left by well-intentioned benefactors to provide security for their loved ones. These can, however, become burdens that prevent new exploration and personal growth. They can keep one locked in a static life-style filled with the repetiveness of lost mobility.

It is sad to see people clinging to their past achievements for security. Sometimes plaudits or prizes won in high school or college days are used by middle-aged people as an outdated "blanket."

For example, there is that paunchy, middle-aged man competing for attention with his young athletic son. Regardless of how well his son plays on the football field, the father can tell him every "mistake" he made, each quarter of the game. He then compares his son's "disappointing" performance with his own inspired exploits of former years. "I'd never have thrown the pass that was intercepted. What ever possessed you to do that?

Don't you remember anything I told you? When I played in the state championship game as a junior. . ." and off he goes, into a long dissertation about the only time and place he ever felt like number one.

Sometimes, a certain home, office, or geographical niche spells security. Others yearn for the security of their parents' home. Paradoxically, some parents, in a very common role reversal, cling to their children as security blankets; validation of their own adulthood is achieved vicariously through their children's achievements (and expected future achievements).

Jean was an only child in the family of a well-to-do psychiatrist. From her birth she was protected from many of the activities consistent with her age. Her mother was committed to making her the perfect child and had great needs to prove that she was a "good" mother. Although they lived just one block from the post office and store, they never allowed Jean to walk there, even when she was in high school. Although the school bus passed her house each morning her mother drove her to school herself. When Jean fell in love and wanted to marry, the mother offered her a fancy trip with her as a substitute.

It became increasingly apparent that this dependent relationship was meeting the mother's needs rather than Jean's. Whenever the mother was asked what she was doing or what was new in her life, she would talk about Jean's latest adventure and her fear that someday her "closest buddie" would find someone to marry and leave her all alone. She heightened her daughter's guilt by reminding her how much of her own life she had donated to making Jean's success possible, and reminding her that when she grew "old" it wouldn't be fair for Jean to go away.

Borrowed Blankets

In much the same way as one can borrow money, it is possible to "borrow" status or a kind of security from achievements of ancestors, membership in a certain social or sports club, influential friends, an honor-society key, the right kind of car, clothes, position, or bank account. A security blanket may also be a church, a family name, or an authority figure.

The common element of these borrowed blankets is their "externalness." They originate outside the self and are usually not "earned" by any individual effort. The person who depends on them for security is doomed to live the life of a "second-hander." This type of person is usually not free to find solutions to problems alone, but depends on others for answers. Self-reliance and independence are sacrificed.

Often inherent in the personality of the user of borrowed security is the necessity to please. If a person derives a sense of well-being from approval by influential, impressive, or authoritarian sources, the tendency is to please these sources. This occurs at no small cost to the self.

When a person tries to order his or her life based on the standards, expectations, or approval of others, growth is usually impaired. When an individual is imitating, conforming, or habitually seeking "answers" from others, the movement is toward self-alienation. Gradually, such a person loses touch with reality and personal feelings and is unable to experience life in genuine way. The security of a borrowed blanket, if maintained, will result in the development of a vicious circle of pleasing and depending on others.

There is no better example of the pleasing-dependent syndrome than Brian. At an early age he focused his energy on trying to please his family, his neighbors, and his friends. In high school he was afraid he couldn't please "the gang." He worried about what he wore, whom he sat next to at games, whom he dated, and where he went to college. It took energy to keep himself attuned to all the instructions he required to know what he needed to do to please others. Of course, such a need left him doomed to failure. Even after trying as hard as he could, he would never succeed at pleasing everyone. The constant approval that he sought from others would always be an impossible goal.

Dependency Creates Hostility

Needing security blankets and depending on sources outside ourselves for most of the answers often lead to hostility and depression because we are subject to a constrictive dependency over which we have little control. Often these outside sources of support live up to our expectations of them. However, they cannot always meet our needs. When they do not, there is a sense of frustration and anger. Our dependency creates hostility. When the hostility is turned inward rather than expressed or dealt with in some other way we pay the high price of being depressed. Depression is often hostility turned inward.

Insecure, dependent people seldom dare express hostility directly. It is too frightening to even consider telling off the needed person. It is much easier to turn all of the anger and hostility inward. This can set in motion another cycle, similar to the pleasing-depending cycle mentioned above.

How many security blankets we need depends on our own sense of personal adequacy. There is a direct relationship between need and lack of identity. Identity, selfhood, positive self-image, emotional maturity, self-actualization—all are synonymous phrases that describe a state to which people often give lip service but rarely seek. Why? Because building identity is hard. It entails an emotional growth that can be painful. It is *difficult* to decide what is really you, as opposed to all that has been imposed upon you from the outside. No small amount of courage is required to challenge the answers of significant others, but it seems that such a process is a necessary, although not a sufficient, step in achieving an identity.

One class member shared an insight into her own personal battle for identity. She said, "Now that I have begun to realize that becoming a *real* person is a 'do-it-yourself' job, I listen less to the evaluations of others and I listen more to myself."

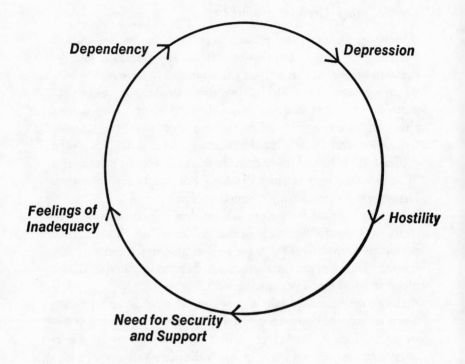

Why Let Go?

Why should one let go of security blankets? What's wrong with being irrationally dependent on someone or something if it gives comfort and a sense of safety and security?

The security blanket we cling to out of *need* for an anchor in our lives does not constitute roots on which we can depend. Whenever our essential resources lie outside ourselves, we are in danger. All external sources of security can be taken away or destroyed by events or by others. Fortunes can be lost. Possessions can be stolen. Trusted relationships can be ended. Social, religious, and professional groups may lose favor, disband, or support beliefs that may become incompatible with personal experiences. Our own inner strength is the only resource over which we can have some confident control and from which we can garner some continued assurance of support.

Security Blanket Analysis

Ask yourself, "What are some of the security blankets on which I depend?" Write down on separate pieces of paper as many of your security blankets as you can. Sort these slips into three piles: those that are controlled by others; those that could be lost, stolen, or destroyed; those that are borrowed or inherited. Now, look at your three piles. Is anything left over? Ask yourself if all of the factors that control and motivate your life come from an external source. Did you put confidence in your own strength on your list? If not, why not?

The items that are left are likely to be legitimate sources of security, not security blankets from earlier days or outside sources. They are probably the internally controlled resources that have been developed by you and on which you can depend. Having a strength within oneself is a critical requirement for emotional self-sufficiency.

Uncomplicating Your Life

Hanging on to security blankets that are externally defined offers only a false sense of security. That false sense may, however, disguise the need to develop internal resources, and thus you will remain insecure in the deepest sense.

Uncomplicating your life is *not* easy. "Uncomplicated," according to Webster, means "not complicated by something *outside itself*." (Emphasis added.) That definition is especially applicable to the meaning of security as here defined, since to be secure one cannot depend on things external to the self. One can love them, care about them, respond to them, enjoy them, and understand them, but one *cannot become controlled by them*. As Carl Rogers points out, there is a great difference be-

tween the person who says, "I love you because I need you,"
and the one who says, "I need you because I love you." Both are
dependency positions. The first stance creates problems; the
second creates support.

One woman's experience leaving a position of absolute "security" (in a cloister) and going to one of comparative risk—but
with the promise of personal freedom—was described by her in
the following words:

> I did not succumb to what was overpowering and paralyzing in the
> lives of many other fellow sisters who had also left the order. I let
> go, moved on, reoriented myself. I found freedom and excitement,
> new growth, new dimensions to my being. I gave up the submissive,
> dependent track. I found my capacity for freedom.

Where Is Security to Be Found?

Being secure is not so much a thing, a person, or a place as
it is an inner attitude of confidence in oneself. It is a hard-won
faith in one's own powers to cope and to survive. It is the confidence to be alone if need be, with nothing but one's own internal
wisdom and strength. It is the security that comes from knowing
you have resources that no one else can take away. It is freedom
from needing security blankets.

How does one give up security blankets and find this kind of
psychological strength and independence? There is no easy way,
but it is unlikely that it will ever be any easier to begin than it
is right now. So, despite fears and anxieties, you can plunge
right in.

Some Steps toward Weaning Yourself
Away from Security Blankets

1. Own your own strengths. List all the things you do well
and the accomplishments you have made.
2. Congratulate and reward yourself when you've made a
good decision—on your own.

3. Listen more often to your inner voice, and less to the conflicting demands of others.

4. Come to view outside supports as bonuses, *not* as things you *need*.

5. Realize that only *you* are the authority on what's good for you.

6. Know that if you find yourself, you may be alone—but never lonely.

CHAPTER 6

Letting Go
of Myths and
Fantasies

When I was in my senior year at high school, someone gave me a marriage manual which was supposed to give the perfect counsel for one contemplating marriage. The description of how beautiful marriage would be if only one could follow the prescribed rules was exceeded only by the romanticism of Hollywood productions. My expectations were already unrealistic and the manual only exaggerated them even more.

By the time I married, my fantasies were totally unreal. No marriage could meet the glowing ideal I had conjured up in my mind, and any measure of happiness we managed to share seemed to fall short of the mark. It seemed flat and routine when judged by my expectation that paradise would be ushered in whenever there was an occasion to share. I felt cheated, guilty, and defrauded. It took me a long time and many hours of therapy to let go of my erroneous assumptions about men and women and to realize that the standards described in my school manual were often based on fantasy. They were unattainable even by the most competent marriage partners.

The above description was taken from a paper written for a marriage and family counseling class by a forty-two-year-old man who had announced at the beginning of the semester that his main reason for taking the class was to learn something about marriage. Though he'd been married nearly eighteen years, he felt he was still operating on inaccurate data and unrealistic expectations. The myths and fantasies he had learned in his youth and transported with him into marriage had led him to the brink of disaster. He needed to let go of them all and replace them with realistic information.

When we operate from inaccurate assumptions we usually end up being frustrated and disillusioned because things don't turn out the way we thought they would. We are left feeling cheated, guilty, and defrauded just as Jim did when he operated on the inaccurate fantasies created by the marriage manual.

As we grow in our environment, it is amazing how many ideas and beliefs we pick up that simply are not accurate. They are myths and fantasies that have been created as a way to rationalize our pain, disengage us from life when the going gets rough, or help us cope with other kinds of problems and anxieties that occur in our lives. The unfortunate aspect is that too many people buy these myths and fantasies as "truths"—and then transmit them from one generation to another as accurate descriptions of how the world operates.

In his book *Transformations*, Roger Gould explains how the process of moving from childhood into adulthood is "a process of shedding a whole network of assumptions, rules, fantasies, irrationalities, and rigidities." (Gould 1978, p. xiii). Only by releasing ourselves from such false assumptions can we escape the illusions that prevent our growth as adult human beings.

It is true that most of us have our favorite daydreams, and fantasy can be rejuvenating. A certain amount of fantasizing about the past and guessing about the future can be useful. Fantasies can be particularly helpful when we find ourselves in a desperately boring situation that seems to have us trapped for the moment. Sometimes being able to escape from the mundane into a peaceful meadow or a refreshing seaside constructed from one's own imagination can be a very creative way of coping, particularly when we *know* that we're using our imagination to help us cope. Instances have been recorded which illustrate how the ability to remove oneself from the immediate environment through reminiscence and fantasy has determined whether or not a person survives an intense experience of isolation (like being in a prison camp or a shipwreck). Just as fantasy can be useful, however, so can it be crippling. It can be an unfortunate waste when one begins to prefer fantasy to reality and the controlled dreams of one's own spinning to the spontaneity of real encounters with people.

Fantastic Price Tags

Living in a world of fantasy can be very costly. Overindulging in it will lead to frustration and disappointments. Fantasies can rob you of your capacity to get in touch with yourself and with the rich resources that reality has to offer. They can do psychological harm by lulling you into the belief that *imaginary* descriptions are fact. They can dull your awareness of your surroundings and hence interfere with day-to-day life. People who fantasize too much can even start to see the world in such a distorted and idiosyncratic way that they beome alienated from themselves as well as the physical world around them.

Not so long ago at a professional convention a behavioral scientist casually remarked, "Everyone fantasizes most of the time." The important question of course is how much time is actually spent on fantasy activity and how much of this is spent on *unproductive* or *destructive* fantasizing?

Unproductive fantasies are recurring fantasies, usually of some intensity or vividness, that consume considerable time. Destructive fantasies also result in an unpleasant mood, feelings of guilt, and irritation.

Identifying Fantasies

The process of fantasy identification begins with a discovery of the stream of your fantasies. For several days *become aware of your fantasy stream whenever possible* and take notes of the content of your fantasies. After you have accumulated several days of notes ask yourself some of the following questions:

What are my fantasies?

When do I use them?

Are they mechanisms for escape?

Could I cope with unpleasant experiences in a more productive way?

Could I use the energy invested in fantasy to change the experiences I now cannot face?

Can I remove some of my reasons for wanting to escape?

Could I make some of my fantasies *real*?

Would I make them real if I could?

Finally, go over your notes and identify unproductive and destructive fantasies. Look for patterns. What purposes do they serve?

A middle-aged woman who had decided to return to college to work on a bachelors degree shared one of the fantasies that had kept her out of school and immobilized her in academic situations for over fifteen years. She said:

One of my most destructive fantasies was the belief that my friends were smarter than I. I even used to dream that we were all in a class together. I failed. Everyone else got A's. These dreams reinforced my fantasy that they were brighter than I and increased my fear of competition. When my friends enrolled in an extension class at the university, I really wanted to go, but I lived and relived the fantasy that I would fail. I was sure I would be an embarrassment not only to me but to them as well. I wasn't willing to risk that possibility so I didn't register. I stayed home, missed the class, felt lonely and incompetent, and failed to learn any new information; all I did was add to my already immense fear of competing. Increasingly, I am realizing that I am in a lose-lose situation.

My friends tell me I should open myself up and begin to explore new areas, but I'm afraid. I guess the real truth is that I'll always be afraid if I don't get going and make a genuine effort to change. I keep thinking it's easier to continue doing what I've always done, and yet I'm beginning to think that, in one way my current ways may not be easy at all. The loneliness and frustration I experience are certainly not "easy" on me. Somehow I've got to do something different if I'm going to rid myself of the fantasy that I'm so dumb and my friends are so smart.

Just sharing her fantasy with someone else helped this woman deal with it more realistically. Once she was able to open up about her fears, she became more aware of them and began to test what was reality and what was fantasy. She learned that there were others who also had unrealistic fears and that there were people who were willing to support her when they understood what she needed.

So often it is the fear of ridicule and nonsupport from those we love that keep us from making the moves that would lead to new control over our lives. If we could enlist the understanding and support of our friends, family, or professionals, it would make the letting go of fantasies much easier. If we can't enlist their support, we need to make our moves anyway. We can't afford our illusions if we want to grow and to discover the excitement of living our own unique lives. Once a person has experienced the excitement of a real travel adventure, just dreaming about it will seem very pale in comparison. A warm body and a shared smile beat illusive dreaming any day!

Common Myths

Perhaps just as debilitating as unproductive and destructive fantasies are the common myths that clutter many of our belief systems. Because they are so widespread and because people believe in them so strongly it is difficult to identify and change common myths. Only a few of the more frequently encountered myths are discussed in this section, but they will serve as examples and perhaps become catalysts in helping you to recall other myths that have a potential for creating problems in your life.

We all have our own unique set of myths. These have usually been introduced and reinforced in our impressionable years by people close to us who are anxious to give us the benefit of their own view of the world and to have us join them in their misconceptions. Because they are important persons in our lives, we often do not question the validity of their descriptions. We simply accept their views and assimilate them into our own beliefs. We seldom ask where their perceptions came from, and we spend little time criticizing them or the results they have engendered in the lives of those who have shared them with us. We almost always fail to realize that those who pass on the myths to us have accepted them as irrationally from the people close to *them* as we are now doing. There is little evidence to suggest that anyone along the way has checked out these myths. They have simply been passed on with a kind of mystical injunction that says we *must not question.*

These are some commonly shared myths in our society:

Money will solve everything. Too often we hear the statement "If only I had money, things would be fine." The notion that money can buy enough power, prestige, beauty, or fame is a far too common one in our culture. Yet, those who have it will assure you that money by itself does not insure happiness. If you have the other essential elements for happiness that money cannot buy, it's nice to have money and the things money can buy. However, self-respect, love, acceptance, joy, excitement, and other characteristics that are important for happy and productive living cannot be purchased regardless of how much we are willing or able to pay. As Thoreau so wisely pointed out, "Superfluous wealth can buy superfluities only. Money is not required to buy one necessities of the soul."

Unfortunately, the idea that we can buy our way through life is widespread in our culture, where the pursuit of money is supreme and so many things can be obtained if we just have enough cash, or an available credit card.

Love conquers all. The reality is not only that love does not solve the world's problems, but it sometimes creates them. Love is not the solution to the difficulties we experience. No matter how much in love you are, you will continue to have problems.

If you believe love should solve all, you are going to spend many hours in despair. Unfortunately, the songs, poems, and stories in our culture constantly promote this myth and encourage us to adopt this notion as a solution to our frustrations and concerns. Few popular songs or movies depict mature love that endures and remains constant despite problems that are as inevitable as the tides of the sea and the natural ebb and flow of love itself.

Some people are perfect. No one is perfect, and the expectation that anyone should be, including yourself, can only lead to anger and disillusionment. Unfortunately, your demands on others and on yourself for perfect behavior will never create the perfection you seek.

Since perfection seems impossible to attain, you begin to wonder why the effort to attain it still persists as it does with so many people. If you are a perfectionist, your life will never be easy because no matter how hard you work you can never do enough to please either yourself or others. Try instead to accept your humanity, and the frailties of others. What a difference in relationships it can make when you can stop being judgmental and learn about the joy of acceptance! Virginia shared this experience:

> I think one of the most important lessons in my life came from an old fisherman in Sausalito, California, named Tom. I had found it difficult to make friends, and it seemed the ones I did make never lasted. Tom hung around and filled in the vacuum. One day he said, "Virginia, do you know why you have such a hard time hanging on to friends? It's because you demand too much from them. You expect them to be perfect and that's not possible. I always figure every friend should be allowed at least two faults. I think you'd find if you could allow that, you'd get along much better." I tried his formula and it's made all the difference in my relationships with other people. I'm trying now to apply the same formula to myself, but I find I'm not very successful. I expect myself to be perfect, and I'm always in trouble with myself.

The world owes me a living. This is a myth that says others should look after you. It says you didn't ask to be born; since you are here and there are plenty of worldly goods, you should get your share—without any effort or work on your part.

Obviously one of the tasks of adulthood is to accept responsibility for our own lives and to stop expecting other people to parent us when we are no longer children.

You will never grow old. Many people in our culture want to be eternally young. They think they can go out and buy a new lease on life simply by getting toupees, undergoing plastic surgery, marrying new mates, or dressing in youthful styles. Despite these efforts we age whether we like it or not. Unfortunately, our youth-oriented culture adds frustration and disappointment to the lives of millions when it continues to transmit to the younger generation the myth that they will never grow old.

You can find final answers to life's meaning. How hard it is to accept the ambiguity, the insolubility, and the inevitability of the human situation! We are always hoping to find something definite, something permanent, final, and unchanging. We are hesitant to accept the fact that life is a process of change and is, at heart, ambiguous.

Despite the efforts of a large number of people and many institutions to convince us that it is possible to know the final answers to life's dilemmas, it becomes increasingly clear that if we are to live creatively and courageously we must learn to accept the fact that we live in an imperfect, finite world which is often unmanageable. Truth is hard to know, and we need to settle each day for the truth as it seems to be at the moment, recognizing always that our perceptions could be wrong. Such tentativeness does not exclude commitment. At any point in time we can be committed to the very best we know at the moment, but be always ready to change those commitments when we must let go of our present stance and move on.

Those who appear to have made the best adjustment in life

seem to have a certain emotional elasticity, the ability to change and to adjust. They are not rigid and absolute, and do not demand final answers to life's dilemmas. They have learned to live with insecurity without undue fear and concern, and have the ability to make frequent and continuous adaptations. They do not seek *the* "truth" or *the* "answer" but rather seek continued growth and a dynamic perception of truth. The famous song writer and lyricist, Oscar Hammerstein, is quoted as saying:

> If we begin with certainties, we shall end in doubts, but if we begin with doubts and are patient in them, we shall end in certainties.

> Too many men become certain about too many things too early in their lives. Over-eager to have everything settled in their minds, they lack both the wisdom and courage to expose their hastily adopted ideas to healthy doubts. They cling with blind passion to their false certainties and too often are ready to kill or be killed for them. In these immature absolutists lies the seed of tragedy. The earth is sick with them.

> The certainties of a strong man are built on a structure of resolved doubts. By the time he reaches a conclusion, he has traveled the hard road of reason. Even then, he will be tolerant of another man's beliefs, and willing to compare them fairly with his own. The man with a civilized mind is neither ashamed nor afraid to change it.

Somewhere life is perfect. From an early age most of us have heard the story that in some far-off place life is trouble-free. There is little work to do and those who live there are carefree, happy, and unencumbered by the kind of worries and concerns that are now a part of our days. We each long for our own Shangri-la where we can escape all the mundane cares of this world and find everlasting happiness and peace. Books, movies, songs, and traditions reinforce our hopes that we shall find such a heaven on earth.

The myth that somewhere life is perfect also extends to the family. Somewhere, we believe, there exists a family enjoying a perfect or "normal" existence, and it's easy to compare our own family life to this vista of perfection. Robert, a thirty-one-year-old Vietnam veteran, shared the following myth:

One of my myths was that some married people live a "normal" life. To me, "normal" was where fathers came home to dinner at the same time every night, and children and parents ate an uninterrupted evening meal together. It took longer than I like to think for me to experience enough of life to realize that my views on family life were *not* accurate for everyone, that most working fathers and mothers with active children have unexpected demands on their schedules that defied my descriptions of "normalcy," and that it was a rarity for family life to be structured and predictable in ways that I had considered to be the norm. The price I paid for nurturing this myth of my own making was the precious time I lost being discontented and depressed because my marriage and family were not "normal."

Someone should make me happy. Perhaps no myth has caused more sadness and feelings of rejection than the one that says someone else is responsible for your happiness. Those who stand around and wait for someone else to make them happy may have to wait a long time. Happiness is a do-it-yourself project. Mary's statement makes this perception clear:

It took me a long time to realize that my husband, Gene, was not going to make me happy. I would have to do it myself. Until recently I really did expect my husband to do things to make me happy. When he couldn't guess what those things were I pouted and blamed him. I used his mistakes as whips to prove his inability to take care of a wife like she should be taken care of. What surprises me the most now that I know it's not his responsibility is the fact that for years he bought into the notion. I guess he'd been told that was his job just as I had been. I didn't take any responsibility for my own happiness until a very special friend really confronted me. She really let me have it one day and exploded a lot of the myths I'd been carrying around. It's a good thing she did or Gene and I would never have gotten back together again. He needed to know that it wasn't his lack of skill that kept me griping, and I needed to know that too. Once we each began taking responsibility for ourselves we found happiness together.

I can do everything. If you believe this myth you will run yourself ragged trying to do everything everyone wants you to do. You will end up exhausted and frustrated, because there is always more to do and people will always be standing in line to make more requests.

You can't do everything. It's a hard lesson to learn, but we all must eventually deal with that fact if we want to cut down on the pressures and live with some degree of equanimity in our lives. We all need to separate out the things to which we will give our energy and to which we will not, and then learn to say no to those things that do not contribute to our overall goals. Unless we learn how to decline tactfully but firmly, we will not only fail to do what others want us to do, but we will fail to protect our own priorities as well.

Too many people are afraid to say no to requests to assignments. They worry about offending others and wind up living their lives based on the priorities of others rather than on their own. This is a "lose-lose" proposition. We need to clarify what we want and need. Once we have done that it will be easier to recognize what tasks will conflict with our own priorities. We can then be more specific about why we need to say no.

Beyond Myths

One of the best ways to replace outgrown myths is by exposure to new ideas, new thinking, and new experiences. The following suggestions can be helpful:

1. Make the decision to become involved with people who don't always share your point of view.
2. Learn to discuss differences. Do it agreeably and with the possibility that they could be right.
3. Examine all new ideas carefully and be willing to question what you've always thought was true.
4. Try a new type of movie or play.
5. Attend a different house of worship at least once a month.
6. Take a trip to an area you've never seen before.
7. Make some new friends.

There is so much to do and so many things to learn in our world of diversity. Take a road that promises you some new experiences and some opportunities you've never tackled before. Loosen up. Be more flexible. Have more fun.

CHAPTER 7

Letting Go
of Games
and Artificiality

BEING AUTHENTICALLY HUMAN is not easy. Indeed, it can sometimes be quite painful. Often it is unsatisfactory, and usually, openness and genuineness in relationships contain an element of risk. Is it any wonder that authenticity is so rare?

Negative experiences that leave us feeling "not ok" can be persuasive incentives for us to invent ways to avoid the hurt that being real can bring. Through trial and error each of us devises tactics and habits that help us feel more comfortable with ourselves and others. Games and artificiality are just two of the many ways we may adopt to cope with day-to-day experiences.

On Playing Games

Games are counterfeit interactions that help us support our fantasies and our unrealistic expectations. Most are unconscious. They have an ulterior motive of control and manipulation. They require shallow responses to protect the players from the necessity of relating in depth. They promote artificiality and destroy authentic confrontation at the level where people can meet and share their commonality.

Eric Berne and others have written extensively about the

Games People Play (1964), the title of Berne's book. Berne has even divided games into several categories: Life Games, Marital Games, Party Games, Sexual Games, Underworld Games, Consulting Room Games—and even Good Games. Obviously, one could add to the list indefinitely . . . Work Games, Control Games, Games One Plays with Oneself, and so on.

The main reason for games is the structuring of time with the intent of an eventual "payoff" for the game players. Many games, therefore, are seen by the players as both necessary and desirable. Too often, however, games that seem to be rewarding can inhibit emotional growth and development. People who become habituated to games may lose any hope of achieving awareness, behaving spontaneously, or developing intimacy in their relationships. Game playing can become such an integral part of living that the possibility for game-free relating is sorely diminished or even lost. One student in a Letting Go class recounted her experience with the game playing of her ex-fiancé as follows:

> Harvey's game is by and large "Sweetness and Light." He seldom disagrees. He is usually smiling and courteous. He laughs at things that should draw tears. He agrees with propositions and suggestions that turn him off and make him angry inside. He supports issues that are popular among the group and gives jovial support to ideas that really make no sense to him at all. Anything to keep peace and to make everyone around him comfortable and happy. When we're alone together, his words flow like honey—and compliments spring forth like a gushing well.
>
> At first I really felt good around him. He was so attentive and so flattering. But, little by little his constant romanticism and flowery phrases began to grate on me. His words began to sound contrived and artificial—too much the same from one day to the next. For no reason at all, I'd find myself trying to shock him or prod him into a real response—but I never succeeded. His face maintained that frozen smile that I came to mistrust. I think if he'd have *just once* shown some reaction that didn't seem studied and polished to perfection, we might have made it.

As game players, we value and attract people who will play our games because they do not force us to reevaluate or restructure the way we live, think, or act. We enter an unconscious agreement with our fellow gamester(s) to tiptoe around the emotional boundaries of our lives. Through games, we make shallow commitments. The only thing we can really count on from the other is consistency in applying the rules of the game. Just look at some of the *levels* of game playing that take place between the sexes. Obviously the goal in these games is not one of fair play or the establishment of authentic relationships.

First Level: The first-level game could be called "Teaser." In this game one offers small pieces of bait, intimations of possible deeper sharing, or other incentives that are never intended to be honored. When the unsuspecting takes the hook the player withdraws the offer and sometimes even becomes judgmental about the other's "good faith" nibble. One class member told of a handsome, articulate actor who delighted in the attention paid him by every small-town or airport waitress. He would hint at just enough openness to make the naïve believe that he had a personal interest in them. After he received his expected response he would react in a very indignant and shocked manner when further involvement was suggested. Later, he boasted of the "advances" women made toward him, without acknowledging in any conscious way his own collusion or responsibility in the matter.

Second Level: In the second-level game between the sexes the game player interacts with some level of intimacy, this time baiting the hook with a larger, juicier chunk of self. People starved for love and intimacy are most vulnerable to this ploy. When they respond by biting not only the hook but also a large part of the line, the tempter begins to pull back, leaving the victim confused and somewhat bruised by the unexpected rejection. At times, this game can cause some discomfort to the initiator as well as to the victim. There can be unwanted, desperate phone calls that invade the office or the privacy of home. Anger or guilt can be engendered when the victim fails to hide the pain, exposing the gamester to some of the suffering he or she has set in motion.

Most often, people involved in second-level games are unaware of the psychological damage they do to others. They see life egocentrically, only in terms of how it affects them, and sometimes are incapable or unwilling to see how their actions affect another. For example, Regina was used to playing games with the emotions of others. She'd played them for so long that she had become totally insensitive to the impact of her actions upon others. When the man who had divorced his wife, left his family, risked his job, and given up "everything" to marry her, made a suicide attempt on the day she had set to marry someone else—the only emotion she could muster was indignation. How could he do such a dumb thing to embarrass her!

Third Level: Third-level games are engaged in less frequently because they do require an investment of self that is quite demanding. Here the gamester offers the object of the game a glimpse of such a rare quality of intimacy and sharing that the unsuspecting person gulps it all down—hook, line, *and* sinker. To secure the catch, every means is employed to completely inundate the person's life with hopes and dreams and some fulfillment. The gamester is able to create a completely omnipresent kind of atmosphere guaranteed to keep the object's mind constantly preoccupied with the relationship.

Once the quarry has been secured, the real maneuvers begin. All kinds of promises may be *voluntarily* given, promptly broken, and somehow twisted into obligations imposed by the other. Part of the game plan is to manipulate the unwitting victim into side-games of "check up on me," "why didn't you call?" and "where were you?" to name but a few. It is possible for a skilled gamester to set the other person up to play these side-games by diligently giving mixed messages, setting up expectations and not following through, and/or describing opportunities he or she has for pursuing *other* relationships. A couple of other "skills" employed at this game level are: (1) drawing very close—then backing off in deliberate avoidance;

and (2) balancing caring messages carefully with noncaring, insensitive statements that will arouse doubt and uncertainty. On this game level, double meanings are skillfully interwoven with pieces of deep sharing and moments of plain speaking until the other person is caught up in a net of complete confusion.

This third-level game is hard to maintain, yet it is difficult and often distressing to end. This is especially true if the gamester discovers that taking the hook, line, and sinker out of the catch is going to leave severe damage. Sometimes it even becomes hurtful for the game player, particularly if the other has enough fight (identity) left by this time to question his or her sportsmanship.

Sometimes these or other games take over and begin to shape and direct lives. It's possible that such game playing, if pursued long enough, could incapacitate the player and leave him or her totally incapable of a game-free relationship. And, as long as one chooses to play games, the discomforts will remain: indecision, confusion, inconvenience, suspicion, and guilt.

Sometimes, in an ending that smacks of poetic justice, those who have played games and practiced emotional noninvolvement find themselves alone, either because they've run out of people with whom to play—or because they themselves have become bored and are at last satiated with their own power over others. Yet, even in a time of perceived loss, they may remain totally wrapped up in their own pain.

Penalties of the Game

The playing of games, along with their inherent artificiality and superficiality, prevents the kind of complete and honest sharing that is necessary for the development of a close relationship. Playing games blocks real responses and leaves us feeling isolated and hollow. There is no honest exchange and, as a result, no sense of connectedness or depth in our relationships.

According to Oden (1974), significant and intimate relationships are characterized by spontaneity, openness, feel-flow, heightened self-awareness, availability, feelings of trust, emotional nakedness, an absence of pathological defenses, intense closeness, and excitement at the simple beholding of another. Games destroy freedom of exchange, create guilt and frustration, and ultimately lead to boredom in the personal exchanges that do occur between two people.

Masks Are for Hiding

Besides the playing of games, there are many masks that we wear to cover up what we fear is unlovable in us. Masks, facades—falseness of all kinds—are used to present a front to others that we want to be seen, and to hide what we dare not show.

In the song "The Stranger," Billy Joel sings about the way we all hide ourselves from others:

> Well we all have faces
> That we hide away forever
> And we take them out and
>   show ourselves
> When everyone has gone.

Sometimes the faces that we hide away forever are so frightening and anxiety-provoking we don't ever take them out and show them—even when we are alone. Thus, the masks we wear to hide "the worthless me" can also make us strangers to ourselves. The energy drain such self-alienation triggers is difficult to measure. How can I share myself with you if I can't accept all of me? If I feel I must hide the "unacceptable" from myself, it is highly unlikely that another will ever get to know more about me than the images I consciously elect to reveal. Of course, such control exacts a toll. It leaves no allowances for spontaneous sharing or unguarded expressions of emotion.

We Can't Share What We Don't Know

Often, the fear we have of telling another who we are is not only related to the rejection we anticipate if he or she does not like who we are—but also to a lack of information. How can I tell you who I am if I'm not really sure? The more we pile up defenses to hide our weaknesses, and behave in artificial ways, the more likely it is that we will lose sight of ourselves in the process.

Since self-knowledge comes from self-disclosure, it is unlikely that we will ever learn to know ourselves until we are willing to risk sharing with another. When we lack self-knowledge, our feelings of inadequacy and self-doubt keep us entrenched in the games and artificialities we use to calm our fears. Unless we break through those defenses into authentic relationships it is unlikely that we will grow into self-awareness.

Superficial Surfaces

Another way to avoid facing the complexities and disappointments of life is to escape into the superficial. If we fear authenticity in life and in relationships, there are many ways in which we can avoid thinking and preclude exposure. If we set up elaborate camouflage, we can hide our real selves completely.

We can also make ourselves unavailable to the disclosures of another. By talking about the weather, news, and sports, or gossiping about others, we can be sure that our conversations with others never reveal deeper levels—ours or theirs. We can be superficially "involved" in the lives of acquaintances for years and never even know them, or allow them to know us (our thoughts and feelings) in any real sense.

One of the common complaints a therapist hears is the lack of connectedness people experience in their lives. Whether it's labeled "existential aloneness," anomie, or alienation, the "hollowness" of modern men and women is often the result of this sense of not really knowing others or of being known. The population explosion and the consequent "lonely crowd" of modern cities are sometimes blamed for this sense of isolation. Many of our clients tell of going for days without sharing an encouraging word with someone else.

There are many offices full of strangers who are experiencing their own private hells. Seldom does it occur to any of these "strangers" that it is all right to share their pain or to ask for help. "Love hunger" is labeled as a social problem, and people literally die of loneliness. The old approach/avoidance behavior dominates many "relationships," and is aptly described by Ken Kesey in his play, *Sometimes a Great Notion:*

> The go-away–closer disease. Starving for contact and calling it poison when it is offered. We learn young to be leery of contact: Never open up, we learn . . . Never accept candy from strangers. Or from friends. Sneak off a sack of gumdrops when nobody's looking if you can, but don't accept, never accept . . . you want somebody taking advantage? And above all, never care, never never *never* care. Because it is caring that lulls you into letting down your guard and leaving up your shades . . . you want some fink knowing what you are *really* like down inside?

What skills have you developed to keep people from knowing you, to keep them at a "respectable" and "safe" distance? What prevents you from sharing your fears, fantasies, and dreams with those you trust and love? Do you hide away from others by hiding behind a superficial surface?

Taking Inventory

One way to take a look at whether you have succumbed to the game-playing level of superficial surfaces is to "take inventory." Ask yourself the following questions and use pencil and paper to answer them. Writing out your answers to these questions, even in key-word fashion, is better than asking them of yourself mentally and giving yourself mental answers.

• Do you sometimes sense that there may be more to life— yet continue to maintain the games and artificialities that are barriers to a fuller life?

• Have you ever calculated your losses for doing so?

• Are you afraid that the changes you need to make might require too much of you?

- Does giving up the games you've chosen to play with yourself and with others seem too risky?
- Is it scary to face the fact that you have a *choice* between Being and non-Being?

Accepting responsibility for one's own pain and joy requires energy and courage. Making the decision to let go of games in favor of a more authentic kind of sharing is not easy. Initially it will not be a pleasant experience, but with time and the development of skill and confidence valuable benefits will be accrued in the form of relationships that are more real, and hence more supportive and nurturing.

Why not start today? Why not let go of self-defeating behavior? But how—*can*—one let go of games and artificiality?

Is Something Missing?

In an article called "A Generation of Zeros," Philip Wylie observed that the banality of everyday life often goes unnoticed, because it is such a common experience. Too many lives are humdrum and used up by the unimportant. Most of us spend a great deal of energy thinking about wanting to redefine our unsatisfactory life-styles but never get around to actually doing it. We then tell ourselves that perhaps superficial existences are best after all. We sometimes even end up believing that it is true! As Wylie wrote, "Too much in our lives adds up to nothing, and we look around and begin to wonder, 'Is this all there is?' "

The first step in letting go of unproductive attitudes and past behavior patterns is to stop and realize that you do not like your life in its present form.

> When you are sick and tired of doing what you see you are doing to yourself, you will be ready to search for constructive ideas and new approaches to living. (Krantzler 1977, p. 99).

Until you begin to feel the drag and boredom of your days and recognize that something is wrong with the routine artificiality of your existence, you probably won't seek to change anything.

You will simply go along wondering why your relationships are so unrewarding. When you sincerely want to analyze the games and artificialities that may be robbing you of a more fulfilling life, devote some time to the following exercises:

UNGAMING

Read over pages 86 to 94 and then use the space on page 96 and:

• Make a list entitled, "Games I Play." Now write by each entry *when* you play it and *with whom.*

• Can you see any reason *why* you play the games you do? What are your "payoffs"?

• Which of the above games did you play as a child? Did you learn your games from someone else? From whom?

GETTING REAL

• Now, step outside yourself and imagine yourself as an audience or as someone who is meeting you for the first time. How do you come across? Real? Or phony?

• Are there people in your life who you feel accept you as you are? Who are they?

• How often are you aware of the differences between what you "ought" to feel or think and what you actually *do* feel or think? What do you do about it?

From doing these exercises, have you become more aware of the various ways in which you have allowed games and artificialities to rob you of intimacy and a deeper sense of integration with the world?

Games I Play	With Whom	When	Payoff	Origin

CHAPTER 8

Letting Go
of Constrictive
Personal Habits

Habits

According to an apocryphal anecdote, the famous American psychologist William James was asked for a short definition of *Homo sapiens*. Without hesitation he answered, "a creature of habit." It is perhaps illustrative of our vast capacity for self-delusion and lack of self-knowledge that we are unaware of the extent to which habitual patterns and structures influence our lives. They dominate our existence from the moment we wake up until we fall asleep again. Habits carry us through the routine of daily activities. Not only are our working hours heavily routine, but many aspects of every person's waking moments are governed by routine and habit.

It is of course impossible, even undesirable to get rid of all habits. Habits can be time-savers, offer shortcuts, and leave us time to do some necessary daydreaming and constructive fantasizing. Many firmly established habits, however, act as a restrictive force. They limit the actualization of a person's potential and stifle the exploration of new possibilities. Habits constrict our dimensions of freedom and often complicate our lives. For most people a change in habits results in an increase in energy and vitality. They feel more alive and function more spontaneously. In many instances their creative capacities are enhanced.

The extent to which habits dominate a person's life-style is illustrated by the following analysis a salesman in his early thirties underwent. (The extracts do not include his analysis of work habits.)

Morning Habits

Rise: 6:30 A.M.

Shave: Same way—use same implements, lotions, same brand shaving cream.

Wash: Usual routine, no variation.

Breakfast: 7:00. No variations. Always orange juice. Always read part of paper. Always little talk with wife.

Drive: 7:40. Same way to work—never watching the scenery; think about business or daydream. Use same greeting to doorman and elevator operator.

Arrive: 8:00. Always on time, although "am my own boss" and can set my own hours.

Food Habits

Breakfast: Stick to same cereals, do not try new ones.

Lunch: Always eat at same two places. Order six favorite foods at lunch. Very rarely order other than favorite foods. Order coffee only.

Supper: Wife cooks, good variety. Only time I make requests is for favorites (pork chops, steak, roast). Never request anything else. Eat white bread only. Use ketchup on everything, very few other condiments. Consume little candy, chocolate bars only. Always buy peanuts (other nuts only at Christmas.)

Recreation and Leisure-time

Television: Same programs every night. (Once I find what I like, I rarely experiment.)

Movies: Take wife out once a week, like mostly comedies.

Party: One every six weeks—same folks.

Read: Paper every night. (Have not changed subscription for four years, although we have three dailies.)

Dine Out: Go to one of five restaurants, when taking wife to dinner-dance (average once in ten days). First restaurant, order steak only; others, trout, and so on. Always one cocktail before dinner (wife, sometimes two).

Golf: Only on Saturday (could play at other times).

Fish: Summer only, same four places—rotation. Same folks.

Swim: Summer only, at_____beach.

(P.S. This list is incomplete.)

Evening Habits

On coming home, always kiss wife same way.

Invariably read paper (sports always first).

Drink milk with supper.

Television (above).

Talk with wife about day at office.

Stay at home and go out only on certain weeknights—no reason but habit.

Use same chairs, one to read, one to eat.

To bed, usually at 11 P.M.

Sexual relations with wife same nights.

Other Habits

Same drinks, same brand of beer.

Buy conservative clothes.

Wear pajamas only—never tried nightshirts.

Attend football games regularly—no other sports.

Never walk when I can ride.

Stick to Chevrolet.

Another set of restrictive habit patterns is listed by a middle-aged housewife who describes herself as having developed a "broad base of experiences."

Daily Routine

Get up. Make my bed. Wake kids. Get breakfast and get them off to school. Husband to work. Fix makeup and hair. Tidy up the house (the same things need doing every day).

Watch TV during lunch. Eat same thing usually every day.

Get mail. Read paper.

Call mother on the phone.

Shop. Get home to meet kids after school.

Cook dinner. Do dishes. Watch TV or read (occasionally listen to records; about once a week, practice piano).

Little variation on weekdays.

Recreation

Movies about once a month.

Bowl every Thursday.

Out to dinner twice a month—pizza parlor, two other restaurants. Seldom try a new place.

Go shopping about twice a month.

Play tennis every Sunday morning.

Occasionally ask other couple to join us for a night out. Usually one of two couples.

About once a year get together with the "old gang."

Ride—go to one of five places or areas!!!

Vacations—Three choices:

        beach, mountains, to see family.

Closer examination of only a few of these items reveals their constricting and limiting effect. Always looking at the same television programs, using the rationalization that "these are my favorites" completely eliminates looking for new and better programs. Always ordering a choice among the five or six favorite dishes restricts culinary adventure and new taste experiences. Being afflicted with too many habits stifles the ability to take risks and greatly diminishes the possibilities for new experiences.

These are necessary for enrichment and provide us with new perspectives and new vitality.

Types of Habit Structures

Many kinds of habits can be distinguished. Among these are the following:

1. Daily routines and habits. These range from the same, invariable breakfast menu to always doing the same things for recreation.

2. Habitual modes of perception. We see or are aware only marginally of the landscape through which we ride to work every morning. We usually look with little interest and see only the apparent changes, whereas closer examination could disclose many unique characteristics that we never even see. As one person noted, "I have been driving the same way for years, never noticing anything. I see things now I never saw before. Not only do the mountains change color continually, but I notice all kinds of growing things, birds, greenery, and construction—I like it; I find I am interested now in what is going on around me."

3. Habitual modes of thinking. We tend to think along the same lines, and are comfortable only with certain set ways of thinking and with our own ideas. We do not like to see them challenged, and we generally resist any new ideas. Our tendency is to establish the habit of letting others do our thinking for us. We are much too prone to adopt the opinions of those who present their ideas in the national media. Their thinking should initiate a reaction of further original thinking in us, engendered by the seeds that they plant, but all too often these seeds fall on the infertile ground of pleased and noncritical acceptance and no further development takes place. Instead, we are left with a pleasant afterglow (somebody else's cleverness, if agreeable, is indeed pleasant), and the idea that was presented is soon forgotten.

4. Habitual modes of feeling and certain routine emotional re-

sponses to recurrent or stock situations. These are called "habit emotions." The greater the proliferation of habit emotions, the more constricted the personality and the less favorable the outlook for the realization of individual potential.

An aspect of habit emotions is learned. Many people, on being offered any criticism, constructive or not, will habitually react with anger and confusion. Habit emotions often result in inappropriate reactions to situations. They extensively restrict the potential functioning of the personality.

Firmly entrenched clusters of habits, and sometimes habit emotions, may function without the conscious awareness of the individual. We can therefore speak of subconscious habits that restrict the development of potential. The habit-ridden individual not only restricts his choices but, more important, deprives himself of new experiences and, so ultimately of flexibility and spontaneity. In the process, the imaginative and creative capacities are stifled, if not actually injured.

Habit Survey and Analysis

One of the best ways to begin dealing with constrictive personal habits is through a comprehensive survey and analysis of one's own habits. Without such an analysis some of the most constrictive habits often go unrecognized. As a class member put it, "We are so used to our habits we don't even recognize them until we sit down and list them." The purpose of a general habit survey is to offer a basic analysis and identification in order to determine where change in habits can be most desirable.

Only you can tell which of your habits are unproductive and in need of change. You are also the best judge in selecting those habits that you feel are most constricting. A Habit Survey and Analysis Chart at the end of this chapter (pp. 126–128). Use this chart to help you pinpoint those habits where change can lead to optimal results in the process of letting go.

Some Basic Tools for Changing Habits

A number of basic tools, methods, and programs are suggested which can be used to restructure or bring change to habits. This list is by no means inclusive, and various combinations of these methods are possible. Part of the challenge of changing habits consists of deciding which particular method or combination of methods would work best in relation to the particular habit you wish to change. Sometimes when one method will not work, another one will.

Persistence and determination are of primary importance when engaged in habit restructuring. President Calvin Coolidge's famous statement is very meaningful in this context: "Nothing in the world can take the place of Persistence. Talent will not; nothing is more common than unsuccessful men with talent. Genius will not; unrewarded genius is almost a proverb. Education will not; the world is full of educated derelicts. Persistence and determination alone are omnipotent."

The Positive Decision Method

This is a basic approach to habit change which is widely and successfully used by many people. It is simple. A habit that needs to be changed is identified. A positive decision is then made to change the habit, and the change is implemented. This takes a measure of self-discipline, a conscious act of will, and a planned course of action. You simply make a decision and through the use of willpower initiate a change.

Positive results in these instances are especially gratifying because they are indicative of self-mastery, and they raise self-esteem. One person described the process this way:

I took a look at my recreation habits. They stood out like a sore thumb. I was looking at too much TV, just spending too much time in front of the boob tube. I decided to make a change and cut tube watching by at least a third if not by half. First, I took the week's listings and marked all programs I wanted to watch. I then asked myself, "Which are the really quality programs?" This cut the list almost in half. I had been watching a lot of second-rate stuff just to kill time. I marked those programs I considered top-quality with red. The rest were out. I decided to spend the "free time" catching up on my reading and visiting friends. I decided to do it, I did it, and boy do I feel good!

The Positive Decision Method is especially successful where a "success orientation" exists, i.e., the person believes or strongly suspects that he or she will be able to master a specific habit with little or no difficulty. In these instances there may, on occasion, be a reversion back to the old "bad" habits. But this is immediately corrected and the old habit pattern is not resumed. "If I backslide, I immediately catch myself. I am even more determined to beat the bad habit." Thus even lapses can be used to reinforce the will to achieve self-mastery.

The Basic Retraining Program

The Basic Retraining Program is especially valuable in dealing with habits that may be particularly difficult to break. As in the Positive Decision Method, main ingredients are a decision, planned action, the use of self-discipline, and willpower. As a part of the Basic Retraining Program, planned action to ensure habit change is usually more complex. A written action program is especially helpful.

Very simply, the person embarking on the program establishes a reward system that is used throughout the period of retraining. This includes both positive and negative rewards. Positive rewards are given for a period of success in changing the habit, and negative rewards are used if the person reverts to the old habit. The following is a sample of such a schedule designed by a thirty-five-year-old professional person to change a habit of physical inactivity—a habit many of us have.

RETRAINING SCHEDULE

Program: Do twenty minutes of yoga exercises per morning, following the detailed program listed in a yoga book.

Rewards	*Negative Rewards*
Following four days of successful completion—buy a book or record of my choice	First lapse in exercise schedule—run around block six times
Next four days—buy a ticket to my favorite play	Second lapse—run around block ten times
Next four days—gourmet dinner	Third lapse—clean car and apartment from top to bottom

At the end of twelve days evaluate your progress. Set up a new reward and sanction system if you feel it is needed.

The most successful retraining programs are characterized by a combination of self-discipline and a well-thought-out reward system. In the schedule just described, for example, the negative reward system consisted of something the person did not like to do. At the same time, however, this activity still provided the physical activity that was the goal of the program. Finally, the person gave himself what were, relative to the accomplishments, rich rewards. These rewards were given at regular intervals so that positive reinforcement could be used to support his commitments. In this particular instance after twelve days of yoga exercises the comment was made, "I am really sold on this exercise program. My whole body feels better. I have more pep and a better attitude. I don't need special rewards anymore. If I should miss I'll do a negative reward. But I don't think I will miss." Success or failure for the Basic Retraining Program hinges largely on making a commitment and closely following the schedule that is set up.

Positive Reinforcement

This method for changing habits is related to the preceding program. It contains all the same elements except that negative rewards are eliminated. In this program, gains made while breaking the habit are positively reinforced through a system of rich rewards that are highly satisfying. The detailed schedule, therefore, contains a series of rewards, given step by step, for progress during the process of habit change. One person reported:

I drank too much coffee—up to ten cups a day. This was really a bad habit, and I decided to use positive reinforcement. I set up a schedule of positive rewards for myself. The next thing was to make a note of every cup I drank and when I drank it. For the first two cups I cut out, I set up the reward of some lingerie I've wanted. For the next two, the reward was a blouse. The reward for when I was down to three cups a day was to give myself a weekend with friends out of town. These were really important rewards to me. I looked forward to them and was willing to work for them. They meant something to me. It worked, and I was down to two cups of coffee a day in ten days.

There are two important factors in the success of positive reinforcement programs: (1) the establishment of a meaningful and sufficiently attractive reward system and (2) not unduly hurrying habit change but allowing a sufficient block of time in the schedule for the goal to be achieved.

Aversion Training

This is a program that is just the opposite of the preceding one. A system of highly effective negative rewards is set up for each time there is a reversion to the old habit. The system of negative rewards must be implemented as soon as a reversion to the old habit has taken place. The greater the negative or aversive feelings associated with the negative rewards, the better the chances of success.

One person used Aversion Training successfully to banish a

habit of "not cleaning up after himself." She asked her apartment mate to point out to her every time she reverted to her messy habits. She noted:

> There are three things I really hate with a passion. They are gagging or throwing up, the smell of vinegar, and the touching of gooshy stuff like liver. I bought some liver and put it in the fridge. We had the vinegar. I set up a list of three negative rewards for infractions. I had to stick my finger down my throat only twice. I broke that habit in a hurry.

Surprisingly, another person used Aversion Training successfully for the directly opposite reason: "My bad habit is I am too clean. I can't let go and uncomplicate my life by letting the house run down a little. I keep picking up after people and looking for dirt." In both instances the success of Aversion Training was traceable to the same factor. On reversion to the old habit there was an immediate application of negative rewards that had a high emotional impact and that were implemented by the person trying to reinforce the change.

The Gradual Phaseout

Although used less often, the Gradual Phaseout method is nevertheless quite effective in relation to certain habit structures. This method consists of planning and taking a number of very gradual steps designed to eliminate the habit. Some members of the classes have also called this "the slow weaning process." One twenty-four-year-old college-educated woman decided to use this method to break herself of her lifelong habit of "having to go to sleep with the lights on."

She began her program by reducing the watt size in the bulbs of her bedside lamp until she had reached the lowest possible wattage. She then decided to put a single sheet of newspaper over the lamp to cut down the light even further. "I added a sheet of newspaper on top of the lamp. It took me almost four weeks to cut out all the light, but now I can sleep in the dark with no trouble." Most failures with the Gradual Phaseout approach are due to impatience. The person engaged in habit restructuring attempts to speed up the process excessively and this usually leads to failure.

The Substitution Program

Again, this program is highly effective when used in relation to specific habits where it is applicable. As the name implies, the main characteristic of the substitution program is to substitute, on a temporary basis, a new response each time the old habit begins to assert itself.

A thirty-one-year-old mother of three children had been told by the dentist that her extensive semiannual treatments for tooth decay were traceable to her consumption of candy:

> I had a passion for hard candies and always kept a bowlful around the house. When the doctor told me I had to cut down on the candy I decided to substitute potato chips, which I like. Every time I wanted a candy I took a potato chip instead. Happily, I don't have a weight problem. It was hard at first, but I stuck to it. Then I stopped eating potato chips. It just seemed silly to keep on eating them since I really had no burning hunger for chips.

Finding an acceptable and pleasing substitute for the old habit is a key factor in the successful utilization of this program.

The Total, or Holistic, Approach

This approach consists of using any of the preceding programs or a combination of programs while at the same time making other changes in your life-style. In most instances the changes are supportive during the habit restructuring. To implement this holistic approach the key question one must ask is: "What other changes can I make in my life at the same time that I am changing this habit?" Changes in other areas of life appear to reinforce the habit-changing process. A new setting often facilitates new or different responses. Some possible changes one could make in one's life-style are: (1) changes in diet or meal patterns, (2) changes in recreational pursuits, (3) making new friends or acquaintances, (4) enrolling in a class or personal growth group, (5) redecorating one or more rooms, (6) taking a minivacation or trip, (7) planning as many new experiences as possible.

One working couple in their mid-thirties reported:

> We decided to make friends at the same time we worked on our individual habit-change programs. We also decided to try a high-protein diet to lose weight. It really made working on our habits easier. What helped most was restructuring our living room. We moved the furniture around and regrouped it in a different but pleasing arrangement. Every time we walked into that room it gave us the message "you are working on your habit, and you are making progress."

Instituting simultaneous change in other aspects of your life while engaged in habit restructuring seems to facilitate this latter process. For this reason a total program offers many advantages.

Team Support

Formation of a support team or support group is very helpful while engaged in using any of the habit-change methods described above. Many class participants have expressed special enthusiasm for their participation in a support team, such as this comment: "I wouldn't have made it if we hadn't called each other at various times and, in addition, met several times a week over lunch to compare notes and to give praise and encouragement to each other." Team support is especially valuable when the resolution to continue with a habit-change program falters or a low point is reached. Team Support is one of the best ways to insure the success of a habit-restructuring program.

Some Major Critical Habit Areas and Considerations

Habits related to four major areas are of critical importance because they often affect health and well-being and because they are especially difficult to change or restructure. These are: eating, drinking, smoking, and sex.

One reason, not readily seen, that these habits are especially difficult to change is that they are closely related to the person's economy of pleasure. Habits related to eating, drinking, smoking, and sex have one thing in common: They represent basic pleasures in life. This is summarized by a succinct comment made by a forty-two-year-old attorney: "I work too hard, and I play too hard. I just don't have enough pleasure. Pleasure is just in short supply in my style of life."

Pseudopleasures

Pertinent research about people's pleasure economy was done by Herbert Otto. One finding was that many well-established people engage in thoroughly routinized sequences called "pseudopleasures." The hardworking husband will take his hardworking wife out to dinner at a restaurant once a week, while a baby sitter is with the children. They will go to the same three or four restaurants and order approximately the same dishes. During and after the meal the wife is thinking about the children and the husband is thinking about his business. The evening out is not what it should be—a vitalizing, enjoyable experience of some intensity—but a pseudopleasure.

Pseudopleasures are relatively attenuated, devitalized experiences that nevertheless masquerade as pleasure. They are a widespread phenomenon. Real fun, real pleasure, real enjoyment seem to be rare today, especially among middle-income groups. Yet everyone needs genuinely pleasurable experiences for the personality to continue its development.

A major cause of the proliferation of pseudopleasures is the encroachment of routines and habit patterns. The pleasure in what was originally an enjoyable experience becomes progressively weakened, but the routine is continued by force of habit. The multiplicity of routinized regimes gradually forms a strong web.

People become enmeshed to the point where, if they notice something is wrong, they can no longer see alternative solutions or summon up the spontaneity to embark on a new course of action. Cumulative exposure to pseudopleasures seems to cause gradual but serious reduction of the capacity for real pleasure. The individual progressively feels that life has little or nothing to offer, because it holds so few pleasures or its pleasures have such a low degree of intensity.

One major guideline to follow while engaged in the process of changing habits linked to eating, drinking, smoking, or sex is to provide as much substitute and, particularly, authentic pleasure, as possible throughout this process. Because authentic pleasure is in short supply, causing a depletion of the pleasure economy, most people have special difficulty in changing habits that are linked to enjoyment.

EATING HABITS

Eating habits are one of the health disasters of this nation. It is a byword among public health officials, nutritionists, and physicians that the prime cause of many, if not most, health problems is overeating and underexercising. Perhaps the most valuable and effective single habit change that can be undertaken lies in the area of eating. Habit restructuring in this area can result in increased health and vitality, as well as prolongation of life.

A public health official is well known for asking the following question at professional meetings: "What implements do most people use to kill themselves in the United States?" Most persons to whom this question is addressed guess that firearms or pills are used. Few guess the correct answer. He gives as the answer to his query, "Most people in the U.S. kill themselves with their eating implements—the knife, fork, and spoon. They literally eat themselves into their graves. Overeating and lack of exercise are the prime causes of both morbidity and mortality." He then cites statistics to substantiate this conclusion.

Eating and drinking usually go together, since most people take some type of beverage with their meals. This has an effect on their weight. Our most problematic (and consumed) beverage is alcohol. The consumption of alcoholic beverages will be covered in a separate section, as a number of specific problems are associated with this generally accepted social practice.

A very prolific literature on dieting and weight control exists. It has become a major U.S. industry. For those readers interested in acquiring healthier eating habits, the following suggestions will be of value:

1. Go to a bookstore and survey the diet and weight control literature. Pick a program you like, make sure it is written or backed by a reputable professional, and then carry it through with confidence.

2. Team Support is especially helpful while changing eating habits.

3. The Total or Holistic Approach to restructuring eating habits yields the best results.

4. Eat only when you are hungry. Watch yourself, because most people consume a great deal of food without ever being hungry.

5. Be sure to give yourself new and different doses of pleasure to compensate for the loss of pleasure usually associated with a change in eating habits. Upgrade your pleasure economy!

To acquire healthier food habits and start a simple do-it-yourself program of weight reduction, begin with the following:

1. Buy a calorie counter—and use it!

2. Keep a "Consumption Notebook" and record *all* of your food and drink consumption daily. Use the headings: *Time*— when you eat and drink; *Location*—where you eat and drink;

Quantity—what and how much you eat and drink, i.e., are you really hungry?

3. Use these Four Key Stratagems:

- Double the amount of time you use for eating. Chew each bite twice as long. Such eating behavior will make you feel more satisfied and make for better utilization of the food by your body. You will *need* to eat less.
- Leave the table when you are through eating. Watching others eat will stimulate you to eat more. This is an almost automatic reaction of most people.
- Cut down and gradually eliminate snacks between meals. Most snacking is for sensual and pleasure purposes and is not related to hunger. Being hungry is different from wanting to eat a certain food. Learn to distinguish the difference. EAT ONLY WHEN YOU ARE HUNGRY.
- To make your portion of the food appear larger, serve it on a salad plate or buy a small dinner plate. According to one study, "seventy percent of the subjects reported greater satisfaction with the quantity of meals served on salad plates despite the fact that they served the portions themselves and knew them to be equal to portions served on larger plates."

4. Analyze your food consumption using your Consumption Notebook and calorie counter. Be sure you are getting a balanced diet. Use vitamin supplements if necessary. After you have identified your high-calorie foods, post a list of these foods on your refrigerator door or conspicuously in the kitchen. Make up your own heading for the list, such as "Danger List," or "Menace to Your Health List." Such a heading can help you keep away from these foods.

Remember that successful control of eating habits, overeating, and excessive weight problems is greatly enhanced if other people are involved in the habit-restructuring program. A number of successful nationwide commercial programs use this valuable resource, "people involvement," as the dynamic core of their approach. These programs are generally more successful than those in which the individual embarks on a habit change program by himself. It should, however, also be made clear that many people have been very successful in changing their eating habits by themselves.

DRINKING AND SMOKING HABITS

Both social drinking and smoking can become deeply ingrained habits, dangerous both to our physical and emotional health. The two habits have much in common, although the ways of changing them differ in some respects. Both smoking and drinking take place primarily in a social context. Many people believe that smoking and drinking confer status and are the mark of the sophisticated individual at ease in his environment. Smoking and drinking are also used as a bridge to communicate and relate to other people. Finally, both activities in the minds of many have become associated with relaxation, pleasure, enjoyment, and recreation. This combination of factors plays a significant role both in the widespread excesses associated with smoking and drinking and in the difficulty people have in controlling the habits.

The social consumption of alcohol and tobacco is not only sanctioned by our culture but supported by a vast advertising network using sophisticated motivational techniques. Of the eighty million adults who drink, nine million, better than 10 percent, are classified as alcoholics. Some experts maintain that the number of people who have problems with alcohol is eighteen million, double that figure. Alcohol is used as a sleeping potion at night and as a tranquilizer during the day. The amount of harm sustained by the human body as a result of high alcohol intake has been amply demonstrated. For example, the brain tissue of confirmed alcoholics is so radically affected that the deterioration is evident even to the untrained eye. Based on the fact that millions of brain cells are killed by a single drink, a colleague has formed a habit of telling his acquaintances, as they are sipping their highballs, "I can hear the silent death cry of your brain cells."

The excessive consumption of alcohol at social gatherings and in the privacy of the home as a relaxant and sedative constitutes an insufficiently acknowledged health hazard. The well-known sex researchers Masters and Johnson have identified excessive eating and drinking as *the* major cause of male impotence. This conclusion is only the beginning. It is not generally recognized that with the continuous social consumption of alcohol a deep conditioning process is set in motion. Alcohol consumption is associated with relaxation, having fun, being carefree. Soon the individual has difficulty reaching these feeling states without alcohol consumption. A psychological dependency has been established without the person being aware that this has taken place. Normal, functioning people at all social and vocational levels have this built-in dependency, which is associated with the social consumption of alcohol. It is ultimately pernicious to the emotional health of the individual because he or she becomes progressively less able to be at ease in a crowd, to feel good, and even to enjoy life at all, unless a few drinks are consumed. A gradual increase in consumption is often noted. This insidious emotional dependency state, which is also acquired through the use of such drugs as marijuana and cocaine, has received almost no recognition in alcohol education programs.

Drinking habits are dangerous especially in those instances where people have acquired firmly established dependencies. The practice of occasionally having a few social drinks is not included here. People who drink several times a week and invariably during the weekends, however, regardless of the amount consumed, can be said to have a dependency. Those who have an unsuspected dependency are heard to make remarks such as:

"Drinking at parties is most of the fun!"
"I always get slightly loaded at parties."

"I invariably have cocktails before dinner to relax."

"When I come home I usually have something to help me come down."

"On weekends we go out and drink some, but rarely too much."

Everyone is his own best judge whether a psychological dependency has been established. Of course, in making this self-assessment there needs to be a clear awareness that every human being has the capacity for self-deception. As a class member so aptly expressed it, "The person we love to fool more than anybody else is ourselves, and the person we are most successful in fooling is ourselves."

A number of lists exist that can be helpful in determining whether a drinking problem exists. The list compiled by Dr. M. E. Chafetz, former director of the National Institute of Mental Health's Division of Alcoholism, is representative:

1. Any individual who by his own personal definition or by the definition of his immediate society has been intoxicated four times within one calendar year has an alcohol problem.

2. Any individual who goes to work intoxicated has an alcohol problem.

3. Any individual who must drink in order to perform his work has an alcohol problem.

4. Any individual who is intoxicated and drives a car has an alcohol problem.

5. Any individual who comes in contact with the law as a consequence of an intoxicated state has an alcohol problem.

6. Any individual who, under the influence of alcohol, does something he contends he would never do without alcohol has an alcohol problem.

To this list needs to be added:

7. Any individual who uses alcohol *routinely* a number of times throughout the week and *invariably* during weekends has established a dependency on alcohol.

Dealing with an alcohol dependency or an alcohol problem begins with the recognition that a problem exists. Read over the Basic Tools for Changing Habits (pages 103 to 109) and select the one that you believe will work best in helping you to re-structure your habit. The Total, or Holistic, Program appears to work particularly well for many people. In addition, the follow-ing suggestions will be helpful:

1. Go to a bookstore and survey what books are available on alcohol and drug dependency. Browse and read portions of books .You might find an approach or an idea that will be par-ticularly valuable to you as you begin your habit-change program.

2. Never go without a meal. People are especially prone to drink at such time.

3. Watch those fatigue states. They are other times of great temptation to take a drink. When you are fatigued and hungry, you need energy, and the tendency is to use the alcohol as a pick-me-up. When you are changing a habit, be reconciled to a possible weight gain. You can always get rid of the added weight later.

4. List things you enjoy doing and do them. This is important particularly while you are involved in changing this type of habit.

5. In this connection watch your pleasure economy—be sure to give yourself as much *genuine* pleasure as possible.

6. Study your pattern of social activities and social gatherings. Think through how you will handle the temptation or invitation to "have just one little drink." Remember that people will accept you even if you don't drink.

7. Keep a notebook or diary of daily happenings. Analyze your own patterns and determine when you have the most need to take a drink. Start your notebook before you begin your habit-change program and continue using the diary throughout.

8. Use the "Breaking the Link Method." Make a detailed list of the behavior-action sequences or *links* that lead to the actual

swallowing of the alcohol. For example, for one man drinking his usual several cans of beer during an evening, a number of behavior-action sequences or links were involved. He listed them as follows:

One: I sit in the chair in front of the TV.
Two: I get up. I go to the kitchen.
Three: I go to the refrigerator and take out a bottle of beer.
Four: I get the bottle opener and open the bottle.
Five: I carry it to my chair and take the first swallow.

By changing a single one of the links that were listed, a habit change can be encouraged. For example, one man asked his wife to be the keeper of the bottle opener. "I told her I had wanted to cut down on my drinking and was ashamed to ask her for the opener. That was the end of drinking a half pack to a pack a night."

Finally, it is important that you are clearly aware that if you have a fairly serious alcohol problem you will likely need professional help if you want to change. If you are in *doubt* about whether you have a serious problem, it is highly probable that you have one.

SMOKING

Smoking is a universal habit. It is estimated that more than fifty million Americans smoke. The health hazards associated with smoking have been amply documented, and over the years more and more research has substantiated the dangers of smoking. Most smokers know about this but believe their case is the exception: "Someone else's health will be affected but mine won't. I am willing to take the chance." This is the rationalization most often heard.

Aside from the severe health hazards posed by smoking, some of the psychological processes associated with this habit have received insufficient attention. Most people who smoke have set up a conditioning system. In this conditioning system smoking is associated with tension release and is often coupled with a low level of pleasure. The low-level pleasure component reinforces and strengthens the habit system—because, as previously mentioned, generally there is not enough pleasure in people's lives.

One undesirable side effect of the smoking habit is linked to the individual's belief that smoking affords tension relief. This belief prevents both a clear recognition of the causes of these tensions as well as the development of healthy ways of coping with them.

The insidious and psychologically damaging nature of a deeply rooted smoking habit is that in spite of the person's rationalization of the habit, each individual, in fact, is aware that smoking is injurious to his or her health. Since the basic thrust of the sound human organism is in the direction of health and survival, the smoking habit sets up deep-seated conflicts on an emotional or unconscious level. It is as if one part of the person is saying, "I want to live and survive," and the other part replies, "But I am constantly doing something to myself (smoking) that endangers my health and ultimately affects my life span." It is highly probable that in the course of time this divisive process erodes and damages the individual's "will to live," which is at the very core of the personality.

Many people are, on some levels, aware of both the physiological and psychological damage that they inflict on themselves through smoking. This accounts for the fact that more than seven million people a year attempt to break the habit. Fewer than one in four are successful. As Mark Twain once noted, "It is very easy to give up tobacco; I've quit at least fifty times myself."

One major reason why it is so difficult to give up the smoking habit is that smoking establishes an organic dependency on nicotine, which can become as strong as some other drug habits. A "nicotine fix" is needed periodically to keep on functioning at a fairly normal level. It is the combination of psychological and physiological dependency that makes the smoking habit so difficult to break.

The following suggestions may be helpful for the habit-restructuring process:

1. A number of books have been written describing effective habit-change programs developed for the smoker. Visit your local bookstore and ask your dealer to stock a selection of titles. Find the program that suits you and then stick to it. That is half the battle.

2. Look over the Basic Tools for Changing Habits (pages 103 to 109) and develop your own unique program. A combination of the Gradual Phase Out, the Total or Holistic Approach, and Team Support appears to be most successful. Two people working on breaking the smoking habit together usually double their chances of success.

3. Key questions to ask yourself are "What other pleasures can I give myself periodically throughout the day?" and "How can I give myself more *authentic* pleasure while I am engaged in stopping the smoking habit?" One man who loved olives kept several jars of different types of olives in his desk. He remarked, "I am really foolish about olives and sample them during the day. They helped me quit smoking."

4. Due to the organic nicotine dependency that is established by smoking, gradual withdrawal from the habit is very important. A number of gradual withdrawal programs are commercially available in drugstores. They utilize a graduated series of filters that look like cigarette holders to reduce the nicotine content over a period of weeks. This reduces the nicotine craving in easy steps.

There are also quite a number of commercial as well as free national programs that aid smokers in quitting with the assistance of professional supervision. For further information write to: The National Clearinghouse for Smoking and Health, 5600 Fishers Lane, Rockville, Maryland, 20852.

SEX HABITS

How quickly sex habits become established and entrenched is a source of surprise to sexologists. These habits are one of the main contributing factors to the sexual problems that afflict so many marriages. According to Masters and Johnson, "One out of every two marriages is a sexual disaster area." It is now generally recognized that even if no sexual problems exist, most couples use only a small fraction of their sexual potential.

Sex habits are usually tolerated by both partners for a considerable period of time due to the pleasure associated with the sexual activity. The pleasure masks the erosive and ultimately debilitating effect of sex routines and habits. One of the effects of sex habit structures is the slow erosion of the quality of sexual pleasure. As both partners come to know what to expect, and follow the same routine repeatedly, the quality of the pleasure experienced tends to change and may diminish gradually.

Based on the research done by one of the writers, certain standard varieties of sex habits can be identified:

1. One or both partners routinely ask for or initiate sex in the same way.
2. Certain recurrent themes or practices characterize the initial phases of the sexual experience.
3. Leading up to a specific sexual practice, the man or woman follows a series of prescribed steps.
4. Intercourse positions are usually the same.
5. Sex play and sexual relations take place in bed and in the bedroom.
6. Intercourse usually takes place on certain days and at certain times.
7. Communication during sex is absent or stereotyped.

In an effort to learn how sexual habits were formed and why there was resistance to changing them, many couples were interviewed. Replies were frank and included the following:

We didn't experiment very much because we just didn't want anything to go wrong.

Sex is too important to fool around with. If things are going okay, why try anything different? That's just inviting trouble.

We never talked about it, but I had acquired some positions and techniques I had become accustomed to using and Joan didn't seem to have any objections.

I didn't want to try some of the positions described in the sex manual. They made me feel ridiculous.

I work hard during the day and it takes energy to think of something new. It takes two to tango. I get no help from her.

By the time I put the kids to bed, I am too pooped to do it anyway other than the old-fashioned way.

Sex habits very often go unrecognized because they build up gradually and the associated pleasure masks the inroads made by the routines. However, ultimately one or both partners become aware that habit has caused a major debilitation of their sex life. Tragically, this realization is, for various reasons, seldom discussed openly, although a partner may be intensely aware of the constricting nature of the habits. As one man put it, "When we have sex we do the same thing all the time!" This is echoed by the comment of a woman: "When he starts, I know every move he'll make, and if he wants some special sexual response I can tell you step by step what he'll do."

To change sex habits, start with a Sex Habit Analysis. To begin this analysis each person writes the following heading on his or her sheet of paper: "What Are Our Major Sex Habits?" You may wish to take the list of varieties of sex habits on page 121 as the basis for your analysis. It is important that neither partner communicate with the other until both lists have been completed. Preferably each person should be in a separate room while doing the analysis. The final step of the Sex Habit Analysis is to compare lists and discuss the following question: "How can we bring more creativity and change to our sex lives?"

An interesting finding from the use of the Sex Habit Analysis was that quite a few couples discovered that they were satisfied with specific practices and certain aspects of their sex routines. As one member of a couple expressed it, "We discovered that just because it's a habit it isn't necessarily bad. We like some of the things we do every time we have sex. All we need is more variety in addition to this." Most couples who use the analysis, however, are appalled at the extent to which their sex habits have come to dominate their sexual life-style. Clear awareness and recognition of sex routines usually leads to the introduction of change and increased spontaneity to the sex life.

The following suggestions can be helpful in restructuring sex habits and routines:

1. The bookstores are full of the latest sex manuals, many in inexpensive paper editions. Why not buy one and then try some of the new approaches described?

2. You already have a built-in support team. Discuss how you can help each other to bring more variety to your sex life.

3. How about new positions, new locations, and new times for having sex?

4. Develop a way to communicate before and during sex. Try nonverbal communication for a change—or the opposite.

5. Discuss the following questions:

How can we make sex more playful?
More spontaneous? More fun?
How can we bring more creativity and adventure into our sex life?

Sex Isn't Everything

One important finding about sexual attitudes is that some people are experiencing a negative reaction to the way that sex is being flaunted in movies and on TV. Several people in classes responded to the questions about sex habits with anger. They were angry at the media for making sex so competitive, mechanistic, and centered around technique/position. One woman wrote indignantly:

> I get so sick of the idea that people have to do far-out, kinky things in order to keep their husbands at home sexually. My husband and I have enjoyed each other sexually for thirty-five years and we've never felt a need to cover each other with whipped cream or try ten different positions!

A young unmarried person expressed the fear that many people have today—"Just how *sexy* do I have to be!"

Generally speaking, the sexual enjoyment two people find together seems to be based more on their capacity for giving, nurturing, caring for, and being totally uninhibited with each other than on their sexual expertise. Scoring sexually—even if technically correct—can be a disappointing and alienating experience. The proclivity to exalt the importance of the sexual encounter has yielded untold misery in our culture. It has equated intimacy with sex and not acknowledged that there are many ways to express sexual caring besides coitus, and many kinds of intimacy besides the sexual.

In a study on marital intimacy by Howard and Charlotte Clinebell, twelve different types or strata of intimacy were distinguished that apply to and enhance many close relationships:

Sexual intimacy (erotic or orgasmic closeness)
Emotional intimacy (being attuned to each other's wavelengths)
Intellectual intimacy (closeness in the world of ideas)
Aesthetic intimacy (sharing experiences of beauty)
Creative intimacy (sharing acts of creating together)
Recreational intimacy (sharing experiences of fun and play)
Work intimacy (sharing common tasks)
Crisis intimacy (closeness when coping with problems and pain)
Conflict intimacy (facing and struggling with differences together)

Commitment intimacy (mutually derived from common self-investment)

Spiritual intimacy (sharing ultimate concerns)

Communication intimacy (the source of all types of true intimacy)

(Clinebell 1970, p. 37)

In viewing the list it would seem more logical if the old biblical adage was applied that the first become the last and the last should be the first. Without a capacity for communication and emotional intimacy it is unlikely that any relationship will last over time. Sex alone can become a bore and certainly only superficially satisfying. Most of us want more from our sexual relationship than just a release of tension, so if sexual expression becomes a boring habit, perhaps what we need even more than new techniques and positions is a commitment to developing more of the other kinds of intimacies in our relationship—other ways to be sensuous and sexually expressive with our partners than just genital sex.

In Conclusion

Some habits are deeply established and enmeshed in the emotional web of a person. They are difficult to change. If you conscientiously tried to change a habit by yourself and have engaged the help of a support team without success, after several efforts, it is well to obtain professional help.

Habit change is one of the best and most rewarding ways of bringing new vitality, new spontaneity, and new enjoyment to life. Although habit change may seem to be a complex process that requires effort, it is one of the most basic moves toward uncomplicating your life. Habit behavior is *learned* and can be *unlearned*.

Remember—Habit change is an adventure that will give you new dimensions of freedom and energy! Let go of

outworn habits and replace them with new responses.

Habit Survey and Analysis Chart

Instructions: This chart is designed to help you assess your
habit patterns so that you can make better use of your potentialities. Habits are behaviors or actions you automatically, routinely,
or customarily engage in day by day. Some habits are efficient
time-savers. *But too many habits constrict and stifle spontaneity
and creativity.*

A change in habit patterns can help you to tap personal potential and bring you new energy and vitality.

Think through your habits and routines in relation to the
headings below. Begin by listing as many of your habits as you
can under each heading at the left side of the page. (Use separate
sheets of paper if you wish and jot down key words.)

*Do not fill in the column headed "Change Designed to Tap
Potential" at this time.*

After you have noted down all major habit patterns and routines you can, review your list. Examine the list you have made
each heading in light of the following key questions:

Would a change in certain habits or routines be of benefit to
you?

What change in habits would make you feel more alive? More
spontaneous? More full of energy?

What change in habits would make you enjoy life and living
more?

What change would help you to tap your potentialities?

*Under the heading "Change Designed to Tap Potential," now
list what you will do in the light of the above key questions.*

MAJOR HABIT PATTERNS OR ROUTINES

Habits in the Morning | *Change Designed to Tap Potential*

Work Habits | *Change Designed to Tap Potential*

Food and Drink Habits | *Change Designed to Tap Potential*

Habits in the Afternoon | *Change Designed to Tap Potential*

MAJOR HABIT PATTERNS OR ROUTINES (continued)

Recreation and Leisure-time Habits	*Change Designed to Tap Potential*
Evening Habits	*Change Designed to Tap Potential*
Other Habits	*Change Designed to Tap Potential*

CHAPTER 9

What's Left
After You Let Go?

As WE HAVE POINTED OUT in this book, most of us have been so focused on accumulating and holding on that we have given little thought to the possibility that we might, in fact, have a great deal more if we were willing to do with a great deal less. Even as we feel the intense pressures created by the weight of our overload we sometimes fail to see that by letting go of some things we might actually increase our most valued possessions and become much richer because of our losses. As Patricia, a forty-year-old lawyer said:

My life used to be jam packed. I worked all day to make money and used all my night hours to figure out how to invest it so I wouldn't lose it. My time was cluttered, fragmented, and packed full of decisions that had to be made and possessions that had to be constantly manipulated and rearranged. If I hadn't met Maria I don't know what would have happened to me. For sure, all my time would have been eaten up with the juggling of possessions from one place to another. Maria helped me to see that if the juggling of possessions took all my time I really had no reason to continue the juggling. She helped me to understand that only by choosing to let go of some things could I find the time to enjoy anything.

Possessions and security blankets, irrelevant past experiences, fantasies, games and artificialities, constrictive habits, outside pressures, and tired relationships only drain our energies and assign us to the role of caretakers. When we agree to such an assignment we find that our daily responsibility for monitoring and managing our accumulations takes the major share of our time.

Unfortunately, most people take on this caretaker assignment with little resistance. They simply assume they have no choice, and seldom look for options. They feel trapped and burdened by the growing load but accept the tedium of the assignment as a challenge to their character and a test of their ability to survive life's demands. They pay high prices in boredom but chalk it up to their skill at being able to get through life without major complaints. "Coping" is valued as an end in itself, but the costs are seldom counted. Life under these circumstances can easily become a treadmill operation.

How heavy a load are you willing to accept? Are you ready to reduce your life to a simple treadmill operation? What if you were to refuse the caretaker assignment and decide to let go? Would you be risking too much? What might you have left?

What's Left After You Let Go of the Past?

Letting go of the irrelevant happenings in your past and of worry about the future leaves you free to concentrate on living in the here-and-now. It helps you to focus on the things that are available to you at the moment, and to sharpen your senses to the point where you can savor things while they are fresh and in their prime. As one poet pointed out, "One crowded hour of glorious life is worth an age without a name."

Someone once said, "If the stars came out only once in a lifetime, everyone would be out to see them." Not only would we be out to see them but all who saw them would remark about the grandeur of the experience. The media would announce it for weeks in advance and proclaim the beauty of it long after the lights were stilled. We would be prepared and finely tuned to experience the stars if they came only once, but when they shine every night we go for months without even looking up.

Our lack of appreciation of the everyday experiences of life leaves us all poorer. What we come to think of as common may, in fact, hold great treasures. We do not have to search for beauty or to wait for some special event. There is beauty all around for those who have eyes to see. Unfortunately, it is not what we have but what we enjoy that fills our lives and as a result, much that could be appreciated is lost through inattention.

How many people are missing their present living because they are reliving the past or trying to figure out the future. Are you acquainted with anyone who misses the warmth of their last precious moments in bed because they spend that time wondering how cold the bathroom will be when they get up? Have you known people who are already worrying about work as they are eating breakfast? And what about the people who miss the beauties of nature as they drive to the office because they are thinking of yesterday's events or planning a memo that needs to be out by noon? Then there are those who by mid-morning are already wondering how to use their time in the evening when their tasks are done. Some even worry at parties about how long it will take them to get home.

When we miss the enjoyment of the moment, we often miss it because our minds are too cluttered to take in any more stimuli. Instead of concentrating on the immediate experience, we are contemplating a dozen experiences at one time. We listen to television, read the paper, and try to eat all at once. We combine lunch with business. A list of layered behaviors is unending. It is little wonder that we miss the messages from the here-and-now. We're not focused. We're losing our ability to concentrate. Martin Buber spoke about "infusing the routines of everyday life with the breath of eternity." He described a sense of the breadth and depth that could be ours if we would give up the detritus of the past and develop the skill of sensing fully all that is available to us at any moment in time.

Our swaddled and weary senses restrain us in a mysterious land of suspension and removal which has the qualities of distance and separation. We let nothing really touch us and become slaves to automatic living, paying very little notice to what goes on around us. Thus, we deny ourselves the fullness of living in the now, which requires that we must be able to open fully our senses and to direct our awareness.

(Otto and Mann 1968, p. 50.)

What's Left After You Let Go of Security Blankets?

By letting go of our security blankets and outmoded habit patterns we can find increased trust in our own adequacy. We begin to feel that we are okay without the "external crutches," and we start to get a sense of what it is like to be in touch with the very core of our beings. We can begin to sense personal autonomy.

The process of letting go of security blankets is beautifully described in the diary of a forty-three-year-old woman who for twenty months took up vagabonding. She wrote:

And I am feeling the rightness of the move, unable to stay in my home town at this point, I am ready to leave. Why can I not do my things here where I have a home and friends to support me? I do not know. Perhaps because here I am constantly tripped up by my expectations, my past patterns. I am restricted to the ways of being that identify me for *other* people. Can I leave those behind—let them go—carry over no mind set about what the limits are? I must if I am to grow. I must trust the process that's going on inside me— listen to it—move with it—not question—just let go of binding patterns and move on simply trusting the rightness of what is going on for me.

When her twenty months of vagabonding were ended she wrote:

Now I know I *can* let things go—move on—pick up what I need— find security within myself—knowing my own personal power, knowing that I can cope with any situation—knowing I can survive —that I can get what I need. Is that not what personal power is?

What a revelation to read that personal power is not always tied to outside supports or dependent on how much one possesses! Personal power is still there, deep inside, even when one lets go of roles, status, and possessions. Only when these trappings are gone can a person begin to experience that sense of personal security described above.

A popular philosophy professor always challenged his classes to decide which state they valued most—freedom or security. Predictably, there were always staunch defenders of each. Proponents of security would claim that unless one were safe he or she could not possibly be free. Others would just as vehemently defend the absolute primacy of freedom, "for without freedom, how could one *ever* feel secure?"

Obviously, not everyone appreciates having the option to do and to say and think what he or she wills. This promise of autonomous living is threatening to many. Erich Fromm in his book *Escape from Freedom* (1941) described how freedom for some people leads to a state of anxiety and doubt which makes them feel insecure. There are those who much prefer the security of authoritarian voices and the comfort of a confining wall to the sobering recognition that they must think for themselves and form their own safe place within. The "security seekers" are usually ready to escape from the personal isolation of freedom back into the security of the group—even if it means submission of their individual selves.

Perhaps over a lifetime there are times when security feels good and certainly it is appropriate for our early years. Decisions made for a certain secure life-style or a particular philosophy at one point in life, however, may *not* fit at a later time. The challenge then is, can you let go of a worn-out security blanket? It takes courage, and only those who put freedom above security are likely to do it.

Read the words of a person who gave up the safety of the

convent for the insecurity of a life alone. Her decision wouldn't work for everyone—but it seems to fit her own new view of life:

> I am tired of safe places and roofs and walls around me. I cry when I think of my years in bondage. I will take what is learned from that and move on. I have dropped the weight of all those expectations, demands, limitations, and shoulds and oughts. I want now to soar; to experience my world; to feel the wind in my hair; to be free. I want to know and to be—me.

The protecting wall can also be a confining one. When life challenges us to redefine the security blankets that now suffocate us, we have some choices to make. We can redefine, and act accordingly, or we can redefine and ignore what we learned. Either choice has its price tag. To reorganize our beliefs and situation is certainly not an easy task. It is hard and often very painful. But not to listen to what we know is right may cost us more in the long run.

Life is more than just finding a safe hiding place where one can feel secure. It is daring to be *alive* and to respond honestly to one's own, unique experiences. One can be constantly transformed by participation with life only when one is willing to take a risk by evaluating what it is that really enhances and builds security, and by a willingness to let go of all that merely stifles and constricts.

What's Left After You Let Go of Fantasies?

Letting go of fantasies will help you to understand that life does not adjust to you; you must adjust to life, not as you'd like it to be but as it is. Getting in touch with the world helps you to accept it for what it *can* give rather than distorting it and then faulting it for what it cannot give.

Doing away with illusions about the world and about yourself eliminates misery from life. It gives you facts instead of fantasies and enables you to deal more appropriately with the problems that are yours to solve. Self-deception only invites problems.

What's Left After You Let Go of Games and Artificiality?

Moving beyond games and artificiality and dropping the masks and facades of self-defense allow us to become authentic and real. Like self-actualization, becoming authentic is a goal sought but seldom achieved. As the well-known poet e.e. cummings so succinctly stated:

> To be nobody-but-yourself in a world which is doing its best, night and day, to make you everybody else, means to fight the hardest battle which any human being can fight; and never stop fighting.

Of course, not everyone wants to find himself or to understand himself, or even to *be* himself. Some are so unwilling to experience their own uniqueness that they mimic movie stars or sports heroes. One extreme example of this desire to lose oneself in someone else's style is the young man who underwent plastic surgery so he could be an exact replica of his idol—Elvis Presley. The operation, we are told, was "successful." He had succeeded in donning a permanent mask.

Being "real" enhances good relationships, just as good relationships enhance one's capacity to be real. If a person behaves like a chameleon, changing with every current of opinion, how can he be trusted? Conversely, when we know that a person will relate to us tomorrow as he is doing today, we can then feel free enough to share our problems in a frank and open way. Also, in terms of personal growth, authenticity is paramount. How can I be more of what I am, if I never know the real me?

Is it possible or even desirable to be always authentic? Is honesty always the best policy? The sensitive person knows there are times for candor and times for diplomacy or even some degree of avoidance. In his book *Pathways to Madness*, Jules Henry delineated between "black sham" and "white sham" in describing various gradations of concealment and pretense in social relations. "Black sham" was described as "a killing sham," used to exploit and even to destroy. "White sham" was defined as that sham one may employ to preserve social relations or to get along with others.

According to Henry:

> Sham is a combination of concealment and pretense; concealment of how we really feel and pretense of feeling something different. Engineered by fear, sham is a bridge between the undesirable and the necessary bearable. The real problem is not whether to be a sham, but to understand when to drop the mask and when to put it on.
>
> Imagine social life as a set of concentric circles: the innermost is the ideal circle of truth, where there can be no concealment; and the out-most is the circle of sham, where concealment and pretense are the best policy and where truth would be gross stupidity. (Henry 1971, p. 99.)

Just as there are situations when total authenticity would be ill advised, so also can the use of sham or games in our lives be totally devastating:

> Learning to live with a person you do not love and respect, learning to live with a person you know neither loves nor respects you is merely learning how to die, how to walk around as a shell, how to deny what you feel, how to hate without showing it, how to weep without tears, how to declare that the sham you live is the true reality and that it is good. (Henry 1971, p. 129.)

The prices paid for the sham of unauthentic lives could never be calculated. They range from psychosomatic complaints to stress-related ills; from resigned detachment to psychotic breakdowns. We must decide whether to pay such prices or to let go of games and artificialities and find ways to assure that we will not become victims of our own shams. The process of finding one's real self amid all the games and artificialities of a lifetime is not unlike the description given by Irving Stone when he described the process Michelangelo used in his sculpting of David, "All I did was chip away that which was not David."

What's Left After You Let Go of Constricting Life Habits?

Many who fear life remain satisfied, satiated, and sterile in a chronic life of avoidance. They take no chances. They refuse to move from the known to the unknown, not recognizing that letting go of constricting habits can leave them free to grow. Letting go of habits removes rigid patterns of behavior and helps to develop new ways of responding. It creates the freedom to be spontaneous and flexible and encourages the seeking of new knowledge about the world.

Today we have more changes in one decade than past generations had in a lifetime. With this increasing number and rapidity of changes, the capacity to be flexible assumes more importance in our human development. Flexibility is one of the most important characteristics of those on good terms with life. When you are flexible you can bend with the pressures, you are able to consider new ideas and to try new approaches to living. You can give and take and create an atmosphere conducive to dialogue. You can accept the possibility that you could be wrong, and this makes it possible for others to feel that what they say will at least be listened to with an open mind. If you are rigid you are more likely to break.

Lucille confided to the group:

There's nothing so frustrating to me as a discussion with someone who is certain he knows what the truth of the matter is. When someone knows what the truth is, there's no point in talking to him unless you agree with his perceptions. After all, what could you possibly say to someone who has the final word? It's like talking to a wall. You get just about as much satisfaction talking to such a person as you would if you were having a conversation with an inanimate object.

Who could not identify with Lucille's experience? When someone is convinced they have "truth" there is little left for anyone to add, and no place to go. The feelings of rigidity and finality that frame such a conversation are not only frustrating, they are exhausting. There are no "payoffs" for either party in such an exchange. It's about as useful to pursue a conversation like that as it is to try and convince a person like Mr. Higgins to see the value of change. Mr. Higgins said, "I am old. I have seen many changes in my life and I've been agin every one of them."

Being "agin" everything must have been a hard way for Mr. Higgins to have lived. Such habits destroy life rather than enrich it. They make it sterile and routine. They destroy the capacity to find new options. Habits very subtly destroy freedom. You cannot make choices until you have something with which to compare, and when you do things in the same constricted way year after year, you do not end up with choices: you end up in chains.

What's Left After You Let Go of Outside Pressures?

When you let go of outside pressures you have the luxury of more time to dream, to relax, to love, to care, and to experience your world in many new and different ways. You have time to think and to "be." You have time to wander and time to linger when your wandering takes you someplace that speaks to you.

What's Left After You Let Go of Tired Relationships?

A decision to let go of tired relationships is not an easy one. When we think of letting relationships go, guilt and a sense of duty to others comes pouring over us in a flood. Do we really have the right to end relationships that have lost their meaning for us or are we just being selfish? Does that mean we have no capacity for commitment?

All of these doubts and questions become even more complicated when the person we want to let go begins to make demands and to assert his or her own needs.

"You said you'd always be my friend, and in this crazy world our friendship was the one thing I thought I could always count on."

"I can't live without you."

"My life will lose all meaning if you leave."

One doesn't overcome such psychologically debilitating relationships without a great deal of determination. One has to be convinced that relationships *should* be meaningful if one is to leave dependency needs that cry for fulfillment or to protect oneself from the time and energy drain of uneventful and inauthentic relationships.

Perhaps this sense of direction is only possible in one who has experienced the joy of intimacy in relationships and who has realized the growth and enhancement that authentic, game-free relating can provide.

Being with a person with whom you can be yourself is so rewarding that once such companionship has been experienced it is not only difficult but even irrational to relegate the precious moments in your life to any relationship that offers less. Once you know the excitement of a great relationship, the urge to let tired relationships go becomes a persistent longing.

Intimacy in a relationship is important. It is characterized by self-disclosure and a sustained affection that springs from total sharing that is both emotional and intellectual, and often also physical. (Many deep friendships of a sustaining and intimate nature, however, never do involve sexuality.) The "closeness" of intimacy may be felt even though many miles may separate the two. So beautiful and complete are those moments of intimacy that many people describe them as "peak experiences."

> Can you believe how I felt to meet a person who was so responsive to my unexpressed needs? I couldn't believe how free, how spontaneous our time together was, or that I could really feel closer to this "stranger" that I'd only known for two days than I did toward my friends of over twenty years. We couldn't talk fast enough. It was so easy and natural to be totally honest. He *really* understood me! I kept wishing our time together would never end.

How much intimacy do you have in your life? How many hours or minutes of deep sharing do you experience in a day, a week, or a year? One study estimated that the average couple may spend no more than ten minutes a day in direct conversation, including the superficialities of weather, news, and sports. Another researcher said that a couple may have a total of about two hours—only one hundred and twenty minutes—of truly intimate sharing in a lifetime!

There are some who are not willing to settle for that; they value too highly those moments when two people reach past all the "thou shalt nots," to touch.

Chances to be understood are important. How beautiful it is when an intimate relationship is achieved and each helps the other to become more than was possible alone.

Letting go of humdrum relationships for the possibility of achieving intimacy in your life is not an easy step to take. It is difficult and, even if achieved, it is not always comfortable. When you allow another to know you deeply and to share your pain and your fears as well as your hopes and dreams, you become vulnerable in new ways. Finding the correct balance between intimacy and isolation is something that requires a great deal of creative sensitivity. The philosopher Schopenhauer likened mankind to a herd of porcupines huddling together to keep warm. If they draw too close, they prick each other painfully with their needles; if they separate too far, they freeze. Only by a constant shifting about can they determine just what position will avoid both extremes.

Life is a gathering and a letting go. It is a taking in and a giving up. There is no stopping the ebb and flow. There is no way to bypass either the giving or the taking. If we are only oriented to the gathering and the getting we are not prepared for the taking and the letting go. When we are not prepared for letting go, our lives can be shattered and destroyed by what is, in fact, a very natural process.

There is indeed a time for every season, a time to hold all of our children and loved ones around us, and a time to let them fly like arrows to their own chosen destinations; a time to develop our talents and a time to achieve career prominence; a time to turn over our status and positions and to share our secrets of success with the next generation; a time to be totally involved and immersed in politics, charities, and professional organizations and a time when we need to recognize the wisdom of moving on to less energetic pursuits.

The fully functioning, emotionally healthy, self-actualized, authentic, ego-integrated self is an end unto itself. It is its own reward. One means of achieving this kind of expanded selfhood is through learning the skills involved in mastering the "what, when, why, and how" of letting go.

CHAPTER 10

The Final
Letting Go

IN A YOUTH-ORIENTED CULTURE many people underestimate the
value of the last cycle of life and fail to assume the inevitability of restricted life chances and to anticipate poor health and
loss of status. Hence they just mark time waiting to be released.
There are some, however, who avoid the despair and stagnation
of the aging years, because they have acquired a sense of at-
homeness in the world known only to those who have finished
the challenging task of completing themselves:

> Slowly, the growing person learns to love, to develop reason, to
> look at the world objectively. He begins to develop his power, to
> acquire a sense of identity, to overcome the seduction of his senses
> for the sake of an integrated life. The whole of life of the individual
> is nothing but the process of giving birth to himself; indeed, we
> should be fully born when we die—although it is the tragic fate of
> most individuals to die before they are born. (Fromm 1955, p. 26)

One can face death with wisdom only after one has learned to
face life with courage. When a person is able to let go of the
past, to live fully in the present, to give up games and artificiality
for honest expression, to sort through the bombardment of
trivialities to find essence and depth in living, only then does one
develop those virtues of identity, fidelity, intimacy, love, and

caring about others. It is from such a base that one finally *is* fully born, and finds the capacity to face the possibility of *not* being.

Death and Taxes

It is not easy to face death as a universal, unavoidable, "final" letting go with acceptance and composure. Even the word "death" is one that we avoid using whenever possible. People say someone "passed away," "expired," "is deceased," "called home"; they say "we lost Joe," or more nebulously still, so-and-so has "moved on to his last reward." Anything to avoid the confrontation with death as a fact of life.

Conversely, we can become so desensitized by the over-abundance of hostility, violence, and death portrayed on and in other media that it becomes even easier to label it as "a finality too enormous to accept," pushing death even further into the realm of the unreal.

These avoidances and defense mechanisms may serve us in terms of peace of mind, but they may also rob us of an even more emotionally satisfying adjustment. Many people discover that they are paradoxically most alive at those moments when they are most in tune with their own mortality.

> The more we can accept the constant pressure of death on an emotional level—the greater our capacity for living fully in the Here and Now, for enjoying and savoring life. By accepting death fully, we more readily accept the many little deaths which occur daily in our existence. We accept the death of our attachment to a thing, the death of a relationship, of a moment, or of a flower more easily. The acceptance of death as a never-ending process in our life allows us to fully enter into the dance of life, the joie de vivre, the child-like astonishment of discovery, of adventure, of pleasure and of continuous joyful unfoldment (Otto 1973, pp. 100, 101).

One class member illustrated how this acceptance of death can enhance life by sharing the emotional impact that a near-fatal car accident had upon her life:

It is hard to describe how "different" I felt about myself and about my whole life after the accident. Somehow, my whole ordering of what was important in life seemed totally wrong. I was more sensitive to how we all waste time—and much less willing to do so myself. I was more aware of the beauties of nature, the common joys, and the fragility of relationships. For a time I seemed more honest with others and with myself. I tried to remember that death was my constant companion and vowed to live each day so I would be "ready" if it were my last. Now, ten years later, I am losing touch with it all again. Why do we have to almost lose life in order to really appreciate it?

Death Is for the Other Person—Not Us

When it comes to being "ready" to die, we are all unprepared. It is not something that we can practice. Being ready, however, is much less resignation than it is preparation. Small wonder that it is so hard for us to be prepared to accept death. Many people never witness the ending of life until it becomes a first-hand drama. It is a phenomenon that we feel happens only to someone else because it is usually hidden away from view—in a nursing home or in a hospital. When we are unalterably confronted with death we are apt to turn away with aversion, anxiety, and a sense of shock. Every time we pass a funeral home, read an account of a death that "strikes home," or see a realistic death portrayed on television, the dynamism of denial, repression, and forgetting is activated. This denial of our own mortality and the mortality of those we love uses up a lot of our psychic energy. But the sense of strangeness and fear of the unknown remains.

Never Really Alive

It is sad to contemplate the ending of life, particularly if that life ends before its time. But perhaps it is sadder still to see lives that never really come alive. As John Henry Newman so wisely admonished, "Fear not that thy life shall come to an end, but rather fear that it shall never have a beginning."

Sometimes there is too much denial and too many emotional and intellectual compromises in life. It is possible to die in stages until—as Anne Morrow Lindbergh described in *The Steep Ascent*—we can become "living corpses walking around." When this occurs, the end of life, instead of bringing a sense of fulfillment and completion, brings a sense of loneliness, self-absorption, and ultimately a sense of deep despair. Alienated from one's own deep inner resources, one is susceptible to fear and outside control. For these people death has not been accepted as a part of life and they may fail to face death as they failed to face life. Norman Cousins, in an editorial about Albert Schweitzer in the *Saturday Review*, wrote:

> The tragedy of life is not in the hurt to a man's name or even in the fact of death itself. The tragedy of life is in what dies inside a man while he lives—the death of genuine feelings, the death of inspired response, the death of the awareness that makes it possible to feel the pain or the glory of other men in oneself. Schweitzer's aim was not to dazzle an age but to awaken it, to make it comprehend that moral splendor is part of the gift of life, and that each man has unlimited strength to feel human himself and to act upon it. He proved that although a man may have no jurisdiction over the fact of his existence, he can hold supreme command over the meaning of existence for him. Thus, no man need fear death; he need fear only that he may die without having known his greatest power— the power of his free will to give his life for others.

Giving one's life for others in the sense of a generative, enlightened self-interest is a far cry from the sacrificial or martyred existences of the living dead. The price of secondhand living, or of not making intentional choices springing from one's own deep sense of self, leads to a condition sometimes referred to as "terminal egocentricity." Faced with a world full of nontransferable experiences, one can either distort one's mind to fit the patterns and answers of others, or one can avoid the despair that results from inherited secondhand answers by searching courageously for one's own unique meanings.

Life as a Preparation for Death

Erik Erikson (1963) developed a theory about emotional growth that posited the idea that for a human being to progress from an egocentric infant to an ego integrated, self-actualized, emotionally mature, fully functioning adult, the crises of the eight stages of human growth and development would have to be resolved and culminate positively in the acquisition of eight corresponding "virtues."

The eighth stage of human development is faced as one nears the end of life—it is ego integrity vs. despair. This is the moment of truth when debits and credits in emotional growth become apparent. The person who has achieved a sense of trust, autonomy, initiative, competence, identity, and satisfying intimacy with other human beings will be able to adapt to the triumphs and disappointments of generative activities as parent and co-worker. When such an individual reaches the end of life there is a certain ego integrity and acceptance of a responsibility for what one's life is and was and of its place in history. Such a person feels a kinship with all of life. Without this accrued ego integration there is the despair, not unlike the "sickness unto death" described by Kierkegaard—and the despair of not having been all that one could have been. If this crisis is resolved, the accrued virtue is *wisdom*. "I am what survives of me."

Ego integrity as described by Erikson is a "state of mind." It implies a character structure that is at home in the world, that is undivided and unimpaired. In short, an emotionally sound individual who can face death and say, "I have lived life to the full and now I love death as its natural termination." (Stone 1961, p. 647).

When an individual fails to accomplish the last of life's developmental tasks and feels the drag of an unfulfilled life the resulting despair is made manifest in a fear of death.

Why Weren't You Zusya?

Perhaps no story better illustrates the tragedy of the un-realized life than does Leo Tolstoy's classic account in *The Death of Ivan Ilyitch*. Tolstoy's character, Ivan Ilyitch, illustrates graphically the despair that results when a person's philosophy of life is inadequate and the sources of emotional strength found wanting when death is near.

As Ivan Ilyitch lay dying, he could no longer deflect the devastating impact of his own fears and unresolved life's tasks. At last he began to face the reality of his existence and to consider that the "correctness" of his life, by the standards of others, might not have been enough to give it meaning for him. His internal questionings grew insistent:

> "Can it be that I have not lived as one ought?" suddenly came into his head. "But how not so, when I've done everything as it should be done?" he said, and at once dismissed this only solution of all the enigma of life and death as something utterly out of the question. (Tolstoy ca. 1930, p. 59).

In *The Death of Ivan Ilyitch*, Tolstoy portrays two kinds of fundamental despair—fear of death, and the despair of not fully having been oneself. Facing death, Ivan Ilyitch vividly and painfully realized that he had never really lived.

This fear of not having fulfilled one's unique potential as a person is expressed in this little story:

> What is my uniqueness as a person, and what is my best self? Rabbi Zusya said many years ago that when he met his Maker he was not worried that God might ask, "Why weren't you like Moses, or Amos, or Jeremiah?" but, "Why weren't you Zusya?"

Death in Life Experiences

It has been recognized by many cultures since early history that the recognition of death in life—the emotionally grounded, gut-level acceptance of our mortality—can be a tremendous factor in adding vitality and a heightened sense of being to our lives. Here are several experiential exercises that can be utilized as aids in facing mortality or as a means toward achieving a fuller self-realization. Some are group methods. All can be modified to meet your own need, since death, and preparing for death, is always a unique experience for each individual. These experiences work best if you have complete privacy and quiet. Preferably the room should be dark, or with very little light. There should be a soft rug or a couch on which you can lie down.

1. Let yourself get in touch with how you *feel* about your own death.
   Can you visualize it?
   Experience it in fantasy.
2. Now, imagine yourself at your own funeral.
   What and who do you see?
   What do you hear?
   Who is mourning your death?
   Are you aware of any unfinished business?
   How do you *feel* as you view this scene?
3. What do you anticipate in an after-death state?
   What do you really believe happens after death?
   Can you get in touch with it?

A number of people who went through the above experience as members of a group made the following comments:

Until you come to terms with your own death, you tend to hang on to things. Things end. Anything you experience ends. When you experience death, you go on to other things in life.

I saw my children standing around my coffin and crying. I realized that I have spent too much time working, getting my organization going, and not enough time with my family. I am walking out of here a changed man.

When I died I began skipping through the flowers, through the trees, skipping through the stars. I could see the earth receding behind me.

It was a beautiful experience. I didn't want to go back. My feeling toward death has changed.

The moment of death was very painful for me. I died and found peace. I feel very peaceful now. This makes my death more real to me.

As a result of my experience, I have more of a feeling of continuity —of totality.

I have been thinking about suicide for the last eight months. The storm is over now. I know I'll never do it.

I died in bed and it occurred to me that I've kicked this whole life away.

I became very aware of my love for my family—then decided, "You did a very good job as a mother." It made me feel so good!

I got the feeling it was going to be a release. My body released itself. My last moment was a moment of great love.

(Otto 1973, pp. 104–105)

Besides coming to acceptance of death on an emotional level, some of the group members appeared to have reexamined the way they were living. As a result of the experience, many expressed an appreciative attitude as if they had been given a second chance at life.

If fearing the death of a loved one is imminent and is interfering with your enjoyment of life today, repeat the above experience by changing its focus:

1. How would you react to the death of your loved one?
   How would your life change?
   Feel it.
2. Imagine yourself at the funeral.
   What would people say to you?
   What would you say to them?
   Whom would you lean on for strength?

3. What do you believe will happen to your loved one after death?
   Will you ever meet again?
   What would he or she want to happen to you during the rest of your life?

Get in touch with your deepest feelings now.

Sometimes we learn how to cope best with life by facing our deepest fears now. Often by facing these feared events and experiencing them emotionally on a make-believe level we can defuse the hold they have upon us. By confronting the worst possible outcome and rehearsing our reactions to it intellectually and emotionally, we often emerge from such an experience with a sense of relief and calm based on a renewed belief in our own capacity to cope.

It's All Gravy

A *Psychology Today* editorial honoring Abraham Maslow after his death in 1970 described his sense of personal fulfillment, his "affirmation of life," and his concept of the "post-mortem life." It described his genuine and thoughtful acceptance of his own death:

> Much as we loved this beautiful man, we did not understand the source of his courage until the last cassette came in. It was a tape about the subject of the current issue—death.
>
> Maslow talked with intense introspection about an earlier heart attrack that had come right after he completed an important piece of work. "I had really spent myself. This was the best I could do, and here was not only a good time to die but I was even willing to die. It was what David M. Levy called 'the completion of the act.' It was like a good ending, a good close. I think actors and dramatists have that sense of the right moment for a good ending, with a phenomenological sense of good completion—that there was nothing more you could add. . . . Partly this was entirely personal and internal and just a matter of feeling good about myself, feeling

proud of myself, feeling pleased with myself, self-respecting, self-loving, self-admiring. . . .

"My attitude toward life changed. The words I use for it now is the post-mortem life. I could just as easily have died, so that my living constitutes a kind of extra, a bonus. It's all gravy. Therefore, I might just as well live as if I had already died."

Most of us have had close brushes with death. We make daily silent acknowledgments of death whenever we ride down the freeways. Don't deny that experience of your own mortality; and don't forget to celebrate all the "bonus" days of your life. Getting ready for the final letting go is more than just making a will and giving instructions to next of kin. It is a continuous process of preparation—a getting ready to be enough so that we can then sense the completion of being "fully born."

Like a chambered nautilus we too can crow and outgrow each life position in turn until at last we float out into the fullness of space.

Epilogue

IN WRITING THIS BOOK we have learned a great deal about letting go and uncomplicating our lives. We have learned from our friends, our students, our loved ones, and from each other. But perhaps more importantly, we have learned how much we have yet to learn.

And so, finally, let us provide each other with mutual encouragement as we consider the ongoing task of
LETTING GO

Bibliography

Blanton, Smiley. *Love or Perish*. New York: Simon and Schuster, 1956.

Christensen, Parley A. *All in a Teacher's Day*. Salt Lake City: Steven & Wallis, Inc., 1948.

Clinebell, Howard J., Jr., and Clinebell, Charlotte H. *The Intimate Marriage*. New York: Harper & Row, 1970.

Ellis, Albert, and Harper, Robert A. *A Guide to Rational Living*. Beverly Hills, California: Harper, Hal Leighton Printing Co., 1961.

Ellis, Havelock. *Art of Life*. New York: Houghton Mifflin Co., 1929.

Erikson, Erik H. *Childhood and Society*. New York: W. W. Norton & Company, Inc., 1963.

Fosdick, Harry Emerson. *The Hope of the World*. New York: Harper Brothers, 1933.

Fromm, Erick *Escape From Freedom*. New York: Irvington Publishers, 194₁.

Fromm, Erick. *Man for Himself*. New York: Holt, Rinehart & Winston, 1947.

Fromm, Erick. *Psychoanalysis and Religion*. New Haven: Yale University Press, 1950.

Fromm, Erick. *Sane Society*. New York: Rinehart & Winston, 1955.

Gould, Roger L. *Transformations*. New York: Simon and Schuster, 1978.

Harris, Thomas A. *I'm O.K.—You're O.K.* New York: Harper & Row, Publishers, 1967.

Henry, Jules. *Pathways to Madness*. New York: Vintage Books, Random House, 1971.

Horney, Karen. *Our Inner Conflicts*. New York: W. W. Norton & Co., Inc., 1945.

Keller, Helen. *The Open Door*. Garden City, New York: Doubleday, 1957.

Krantzler, Mel. *Learning to Love Again*. New York: Thomas Y. Crowell Co., 1977.

Liebman, Joshua Loth. *Peace of Mind*. New York: Simon and Schuster, 1946.

Lindbergh, Anne Morrow. *Gift from the Sea*. New York: Pantheon Books, Inc., 1955.

Magoun, F. Alexander. *Living a Happy Life*. New York: Harper Brothers, 1960.

Maier, Henry W. *Three Theories of Child Development.* New York: Harper & Row, 1965.

Moustakas, Clark. *Individuality and Encounter.* Cambridge, Mass.: Howard A. Doyle, 1968.

Oden, Thomas C. *Game Free: A Guide to the Meaning of Intimacy.* New York: Harper & Row, Publishers, 1974.

Otto, Herbert A. *Group Methods to Actualize Human Potential.* Beverly Hills: The Holistic Press, 1973.

Otto, Herbert A., and Mann, John. *Ways of Growth.* New York: Grossman Publishers, 1968.

Overstreet, Harry and Bonaro. *Mind Goes Forth.* New York: Norton Publishing Co., 1956.

Overstreet, Harry and Bonaro. *The Mature Mind.* New York: Franklin Watts, Inc., 1965.

Pearce, Joseph C. *The Magical Child.* New York: E. P. Dutton & Co., 1977.

Peele, Stanton. *Love and Addiction.* New York: Taplinger Publishing Co., 1975.

Rhoades, Winfred. *Have You Lost God?* New York: Lippincott, 1941.

Schweitzer, Albert. *Out of My Life and Thought.* New York: The New American Library, 1953.

Sheehy, Gail. *Passages.* New York: E. P. Dutton & Co., Inc., 1976.

Shostrom, Everett, and Kavanaugh, James. *Between Man and Woman.* Los Angeles: Nash Publishing, 1971.

Smyth, J. Paterson. *How God Inspired The Bible.* London: Ren & Inchbould, 1910.

Steiner, Claude M. *Scripts People Live.* New York: Grove Press, Inc., 1974.

Stone, Irving. *The Agony and the Ecstasy.* New York: Doubleday & Co., Inc., 1961.

Thoreau, Henry David. *Walden.* New York: Walter J. Black, Inc., 1942.

Tolstoy, Count Leo. *The Death of Ivan Ilyitch.* New York: The Modern Library, ca. 1930.

Wylie, Philip. "A Generation of Zeroes." *This Week* magazine (February 5, 1967).